THE VOID

Why do I Hurt or Feel Uneasy Inside?

Wendy Haslam

AuthorHouse™ UK Ltd.
500 Avebury Boulevard
Central Milton Keynes, MK9 2BE
www.authorhouse.co.uk
Phone: 08001974150

First published by AuthorHouse 7/13/2009

ISBN: 978-1-4389-9600-4 (sc)

Library of Congress Control Number: 2009905946

This book is printed on acid-free paper.

THE VOID

Why do I Hurt or Feel Uneasy Inside?

Wendy Haslam

authorHOUSE®

AuthorHouse™ UK Ltd.
500 Avebury Boulevard
Central Milton Keynes, MK9 2BE
www.authorhouse.co.uk
Phone: 08001974150

First published by AuthorHouse 7/13/2009

ISBN: 978-1-4389-9600-4 (sc)

Library of Congress Control Number: 2009905946

This book is printed on acid-free paper.

The Void

A Journey into Hidden Pain

"Why do I hurt or feel uneasy inside?"
This book explores why and helps you to
find healing

Acknowledgements

For editing, and offering professional insights, overview, and encouragement

I thank the following:

Patricia Hellier – SRN, RSCN, RNCT, Dip CPC

Linda Staines – MSc, Family and Systemic Psychotherapist

For my children

Mary, Michael, and Sarah

My four lasting bequests to you:

God's love, my love, roots, and wings.

Fly well, firmly rooted in love.

Contents

FOREWORD

At the beginning of the twenty-first century, it appears to many that more people than ever are in need of psychological and emotional support. Thankfully, more people than ever are rising to the challenge of giving it. Meanwhile, to comply with regulations from the European Union, counselling organisations are insisting that those who are drawn to 'help others' must be trained to a much higher standard than in the past.

For insights into how and why people can be hurting, and how they can be safely helped, this book is timely. Timely because many do not know how to find the help they need or what that help entails. Timely, indeed, because very unfortunately some of the help that is available can perpetuate the very damage it endeavours to heal.

The insights Wendy shares are drawn from many years of experience both as a counsellor and within the ministry of healing. In an empathic and gentle way, she walks us through a range of situations and events that may have caused such pain as to leave a deep 'void'. This void robs a person of their joy, curiosity, health, and relationships. Sadly, some people find life to be a struggle but have no idea why because the cause of their pain is not evident. They believe that life is just as they see and feel it – painful. They build walls of defence around and within themselves in order to guard against the hurt inside. Unfortunately, this prevents them from experiencing life in all its abundance.

This book is ideal, too, for those who are trained or hope to train as professional counsellors. Wendy clearly describes the process by which one can come alongside a person in order to address and therefore facilitate healing. She warns of the damage that can be done by well meaning people who have the best interests of people at heart but have not been specifically trained for the task. By not fully understanding the emotional and psychological processes they are dealing with, both the one being assisted and the one doing the assisting may not realise the impact of the process of therapeutic help.

Nevertheless, the need for professional counsellors and those who work in a church context is great and becoming greater as the pressures of modern life become too much for so many. This book endeavours to encourage those who are drawn to helping others, as well as showing how the broken hearted may find healing.

JANE DEAN
BA (HONS) in Psychology, Exeter University
Postgraduate diploma in Counselling, Bath Spa University
Further Education teacher's certificate

Preface

A Journey into Hidden Pain

A book exploring healing and the hurts that we carry

This book is written for a range of readers. It may be seen as a self help book exploring and gaining insight as to why you may feel that your life is blocked or uncomfortable. Counsellors and Therapists will find some slightly different thinking and ways to approach certain situations. This may be so too for Pastoral Carers as they seek to establish safe practice and lastly to students who wish to further their thinking in a range of therapeutic areas.

We all bring 'baggage' from the past. By this I mean events that have shaped our thinking, responses and actions in every day life. For the most part we deal with difficult relationships and events in life, but some people realise that they have not been able to resolve certain situations. As a result, their everyday actions, emotions and feelings cause them difficulty in their daily life. If they are willing to discover why they feel, think, and act as they do and will consider finding the underlying cause, then this is the book for them. It will require them to look at their lives and their journey, the good and the bad and hurtful parts that they have experienced. The book will take them on a voyage to discover possible life events that may have caused inner scars. Having discovered that scar or scars – their place of hurt that I speak of as their *void* – they will then know how best to seek an informed way forward.

Having worked as a clinical counsellor (therapist) for some twenty-five years, first within the National Health Service and then in my own private practice, I have grown in my understanding of the pain that so many of us carry within.

Trained initially as a person-centred counsellor, I have enlarged my understanding of the different models of counselling, entered into the world of counselling psychology, worked with a wide range of issues including abuse and eating disorders, and have been challenged by the wholeness – the body, mind, and spirit – of each person I see. I have offered workshops and spoken at conferences over the years on a range of topics including self-awareness and communication, eating disorders, inner healing, and on finding the inner void, which is the thinking behind this book.

I use an integrated approach for counselling based on the person-centred core principals. The psychodynamic approach has been used to bring unconscious drives or defences into conscious awareness. Cognitive therapy has been used to help if the messages from the person's earlier life are leading to self-defeating or self-destructive thought patterns or behaviours.

What we are trying to do is to find out what works for the individual who seeks help rather than trying to fit that person into one framework or model. Having considered a range of life experiences, the book moves on to helping the person to explore any inner hurt within and to understand what that void is about. The final step is to find a healing way forward so that the person can continue their journey through life, not only healed up but also wiser and matured as an individual.

I offer my thanks to family and friends who have journeyed with me, especially my own family. Thanks also go to those who have supervised my practice over the years. I also thank the many who came to me seeking professional help and who trusted me to travel with them to find their void of inner pain. I find great joy in seeing them discover the cause of their hurts so they can travel on in life with a lighter load. I trust that I may be able to help many more on their journeys of discovery and healing.

Most of all, I thank God who has led me forth on my own journey of discovery. I never fail to marvel at the intricate ways we are woven together and at the robustness, yet fragility, of body, mind and spirit.

I came to an understanding of faith in my early twenties as a result of being physically healed. At that time, I had no understanding of healing and, indeed, did not believe such things took place. My view of life changed as a result of the healing, and I was eager to learn more. I began to see the different types of hurt that may come our way in life. As I began to see this more clearly, I was able to apply psychology to my understanding of healing. I thus worked with the different strands to try to make sense of this part of life. Over the years, I realised that healing involved not just the physical but also the mind and the spirit. In my case, my body was healed, and that propelled me into a spiritual faith. I then engaged my mind, and this book is the result of years of observation, training, and practice in a variety of therapeutic settings on three continents: Africa, the United States, and the UK.

I have drawn upon real situations in the case histories mentioned in the book but names and situations have been changed radically to ensure confidentiality.

My desire is that this book may be the start of a healing journey for many. You may have a faith, but, if you do not or are searching for something more in life, as you read, I hope that a sense of awakening may dawn and that you will move forward in body, mind and spirit.

Chapter One

The Void in Relation to Inner Healing

As each new life enters the world; it is the start of a unique journey for that little person after having that safe haven inside the womb for some nine months. As we progress through this book, we shall be thinking about the journey that we all make as we move through our lives and about the idea of loss. Loss starts at birth. A mother's womb is safe and warm and provides all that is needed. It is quite a shock for that little baby to lose that place of safety. Once born into the world, in order to survive the little one has to gasp for air, find nourishment, and hopefully be given bodily comfort.

As the journey continues, any number of things may interrupt the flow and cause some sort of hurt or loss to that little being.

As I have journeyed with individuals in a therapeutic setting, I have become increasingly aware of the inner pain and of what I call 'the void', that place that hurts in their lives. Simply being in the world has created this void. It may result from natural events in an individual's life or from accidents; it may result from deliberate harm or even self-harm. The reasons are numerous and complex.

Having considered a range of life experiences, the book moves to helping you to explore any inner hurt within you and to understand what has caused your void. It will then lead you forward on the road to healing the hurt.

What Do We Mean By the Hurting Voids in Our Lives?

Put another way: are we thinking here about past hurts that have left some sort of inner scar? If that is the case, is it wise to disturb memories that have been buried away? Should we disturb that scar memory? Should we look into that void?

We are all hurt as we journey through life but for some, the depth and extent of the hurt will have left a scar deep inside them. It may not simply be one instance of hurt. Some people experience hurt upon hurt, and one day the pile just gets too big, and they react in some way.

In response to the question, 'Is it wise to disturb such scars?' ask yourself the question, 'Rather than me setting out to disturb them, are they already disturbing me?' This is why so many people seek help. Their cry is that they feel a discomfort or a pain. To different degrees, their lives are being shaped in an uncomfortable way because of emotional scars. This acknowledged, have they – might you have – the courage to risk confronting the causes and reasons for those inner scars? Can you look into the void?

To confront the cause takes courage. It is the place you would rather avoid than confront. For most of the time, you may well be able to keep the void away, to push it down deep within. Yet when you least want it, it comes back to throw you into pain and discomfort. It prevents you from living your life to the full.

You may have visited that place, your void, and thought and hoped that it would stop hurting. But it has not. It just will not go away. You then encounter other situations that build upon that inner scar, your void. When this happens, you increase your defence walls in order to survive. In the end, however, these defensive walls curtail your freedom. You thus become a victim to past hurts. This book will help you to explore and identify any voids in your life. Once you have identified that hurting space within you, that void, light may then come in and the process of dealing with that hurt may start. Once we are able to pinpoint why we feel as we feel, we are on our journey to a very much more comfortable place. The getting there is often difficult but you will begin to see shafts of light. It may feel a little like walking through a dark wood with the leaves preventing much light from coming in. Here and there as you walk, you will see a shaft of light. That shaft of light will keep you going. The final step will be to fill the void with light, with healing and love.

Understanding Loss

To understand and appreciate loss more fully we need to explore attachment. Attachment is an emotional bond to another person. Psychologist John

Bowlby was the first attachment theorist. He presented his first formal statement of the attachment theory to the British Psychoanalytic Society in London in three, now classic, papers: "The Nature of the Child's Tie to His Mother" (1958), "Separation Anxiety" (1959), and "Grief and Mourning in Infancy and Early Childhood" (1960).

These three papers, along with two others, represent the first basic blueprint of attachment theory (Bowlby, J. 1969/1982, *Attachment and Loss, Vol. 1: Attachment.* New York: Basic Books).

Bowlby believed that the earliest bonds formed by children with their principal care- givers have a tremendous impact that continues throughout life. According to Bowlby, attachment also serves to keep the infant close to the principal care giver, thus improving the child's chances of survival.

The central theme of attachment theory is that care givers who are available and responsive to their infant's needs establish a sense of security. The infant knows that the care giver is dependable, and this creates a secure base from which the child can then explore the world.

In the 1970s, psychologist Mary Ainsworth expanded greatly upon Bowlby's original work. Her groundbreaking work in her "Strange Situation" study revealed the profound effects of attachment on behaviour. In this study, researchers observed children between the ages of 12 and 18 months as they responded to a situation in which they were briefly left alone and then reunited with their principal care givers (Ainsworth, 1978). Based upon the responses the researchers observed, Ainsworth described three major styles of attachment: secure attachment, ambivalent-insecure attachment, and avoidant-insecure attachment.

Later, researchers Main and Solomon (1986) added a fourth attachment style called disorganised-insecure attachment, based upon their own research.

Let us see how this works out in everyday life. To do so we need to return to the infant stage. Infant survival depends upon care. The baby will thus bond with its principal care giver. A baby has the innate capacity to communicate its needs. The cry of a baby triggers a reaction in the carer. The baby, we hope, then receives care. The trigger of the cry has evoked a response.

We may then see that, with such attachment, separation from the principal care givers evokes a strong anxiety reaction in the infant. This emotional response to separation in the infant stage may remain as a response which surfaces in adulthood. There may lie deep within the adult a vague feeling that something needs to be restored in them. This sort of feeling has been expressed during therapeutic sessions. In such cases, it is often discovered that there had indeed been some sort of separation when the adult was an infant.

Consider Bowlby's[1] thinking that separation

---

1 Bowlby, J. (1969/1982). *Attachment and Loss, Vol. 1: Attachment.* New York: Basic Books

anxiety is experienced when attachment behaviour is activated. The challenge for the therapist is to meet the individual in their feelings of unease and distress and other emotions. The therapeutic process then begins to take place as the therapist offers a secure base from which to work towards healing.

Bowlby's work was a major contribution to academic thinking about the development of attachment and affectional bonds, and the consequences of their disruption. We have seen how others, including Mary D. Ainsworth, continued this work and thinking. Her research and writings have made a major contribution to our understanding of attachment. They extend the thinking beyond western societies and infancy to show that these findings are also true in many other cultures and in endangered populations. Quality of attachment has been a key variable in developmental research during the last two decades. Even though attachment is relevant to all cultures and humans of all ages, the majority of research has focused on middle-class infants in Anglicised cultures. The expansion of the attachment classificatory system beyond its roots in infancy to a broad range of cultures is, among other factors, what differentiates Crittenden's work from other work on attachment. (See The Organization of Attachment Relationships Maturation, Culture, and Context, edited by Patricia McKinsey Crittenden, Angelika Hartl Claussen. 2000 Cambridge University Press.)

So let us now go back to the development

of attachment and affectional bonds and the consequences of their disruption. Loss and grief go hand in hand when there is disruption of this kind. This is when a void may be discovered.

Looking at the infant and childhood stage, we consider those times of separation between the principal care giver and small child caused by any number of reasons. These may range from short periods as a result of illness or other unavoidable happenings, which for the child may seem an eternity, to the death of the principal care giver. More everyday losses like the loss of a special toy, the loss of a pet, when a child changes class at school, when a friend moves away, and so on, may all cause a child to experience a sense of loss or grief when such events take place.

Loss is a normal part of life and to react to the loss is equally normal. Children experience loss just as adults do, and must be allowed to react and show their emotions in a natural way.

Before looking at the voids in our lives caused by loss, let us consider the phases of separation response as described by Bowlby.

Take a small toddler. We shall think of the principal care giver in this instance as the mother. She, the mother, has been and still is the constant stability and security in that little one's life. Then one day, she has to be absent for several days. This is a frequent situation because this is just the sort of stage in a toddler's life when the mother may have another baby, so the mother may have to be absent. The toddler protests by crying. He or she may become quite angry, and these feelings are all related to separation anxiety. Then fear and anger drive the toddler and he or she screams.

Unless the child can be consoled, either by the principal care giver's return or by a safe mother substitute who may provide comfort, such as the father or a granny, the child may experience despair, the sort of despair related to grief and mourning.

The toddler is grieving the loss of the one who provides security and makes life physically as well as emotionally comfortable. A safe and secure relationship can be re-established either by the return of the mother or by a visit to the mother in hospital, or with the continued care and love of the mother substitute. If the little one cannot find the comfort needed, sadness then becomes their dominant emotional response. The crying is a much deeper cry; possibly even a sob; sometimes, it may even be a silence.

The toddler then moves into what we describe as detachment or denial. This is a defence wall in the making. The child seems to return to a near normal state where she or he is now able to cope with the loss and continues with life. This is an acceptance of the loss. This is not a 'getting over' the loss but, rather, a way of coping. We talk of our heart being 'broken'. The child has experienced a deep sadness, but has become able to cope and appears, on the face of it, to be moving on in life. The little one's life has 'fallen apart', as we adults might say, and when the family's life returns to normal, the child returns to that routine as well but having undergone new emotional experiences.

I don't want this illustration to send any expectant mother into a panic. It is quite normal to have a time of separation from your child or children when you have another baby. Simply put into place the substitute carers for them as you would at other times. No small child should be totally dependent upon the mother alone in any case. I am using this as an example that we can all relate to by way of demonstration.

But imagine what a toddler may go through if, for instance, they are left suddenly, if the mother has a long period of time in hospital, and it is not possible for them to see her. Clearly the love and security of known people are crucial to the little one at that time. Also, to give the child an explanation of where Mummy is and reassurance that she will come back is important, even if you think your words will not be fully understood.

This concept of having fallen apart and coming back in a new way will run throughout this book. As you identify losses in your life, as an infant, child, or adult, you will be able to follow the possible stages that you went through. I hope that, as you read this book, you will be enabled to identify parts of your life that are uncomfortable to you. Note areas that seem to cause you hurt and pain and anxiety. Observe your reactions. You may then start to understand your walls of defence. By a wall of defence, I mean the action that you take internally to avoid a situation, to block it out, or to escape from it in some way. This will lead you on in your understanding of the inner hurt that has been caused as a result of losses in your life. You will then be in a position to heal the hurt. This usually takes time. Healing is a process. One needs to understand, talk, and ponder the causes and reasons of the initial hurt.

There may be a need for forgiveness. You will then start to be able to face up to the consequences of the hurt and loss from the past. You will start to recognise your defence walls and your defence mechanisms and to understand them in a new light.

Defence walls have become sturdy and safe. To take them away will seem very risky and unsafe. Hence, it will take time working with a professional therapist to work your way forward, dismantling those walls brick by brick. You will then learn how to cope and live life in a new way with a new sense of freedom.

I offer you another example: change in your physical health is a loss and causes a void. The loss may be dramatic or it may be gradual. Dramatic loss would come through sudden and violent physical damage to your body: a road traffic accident, a climbing accident, being a victim of crime, having a stroke, a sports-related injury, and so on. Suddenly you are not master of your body; it won't move as it once did. The force of such a happening will create a shock-filled void that needs to be addressed. However, in the concern to deal with the physical problem, all too often those who experience such a situation are never able to look at the initial trauma. They are taken over by the professionals, who map out each step of their day as they are helped to 'recover'. The process of recovery is quite new territory for a person: they have never travelled such a road before. One day you find yourself – really find yourself – with the new you. Rather than finding the person you once were, you find a stranger. You are bemused. How did you reach this point? How do you live with the new you?

As you gain new insights into past hurts, you will begin to change. Your reactions to situations and people will change. There may be some reluctance when this starts to happen; you may be tempted to draw back. You are discovering a new way of acting and reacting, but it may feel unsafe. Defence walls that have protected you so well for possibly many years are no longer part of you. They are indeed being dismantled brick by brick. As you continue to look at the loss within the void, you will discover how strong your emotions can be. Out of this whole process comes the matter of inner healing. This may be a new term to some readers and a familiar one to others.

What Do We Mean by Inner Healing?

To explain inner healing: we recognise that inner hurts are caused by past hurts catching up with us in our present life. Those inner hurts may well be preventing us from leading our life to the full. Something is holding us back: we lack confidence to move forward as perhaps once we did; we sense an anxiety deep within us; we feel a pain deep within but cannot put our finger on the cause of the pain. It is often complex, and we may well experience physical pain as a result of our inner pain.

Again and again, the interplay between the physical and the emotional can be seen. Our spiritual state will also be touched by this interplay. To add to the complexities of this situation, some physical symptoms may be in place to act as a defence wall against any attack on the vulnerable inner hurt.

We shall be holding onto, and working with, the concept of inner healing as we look at situations that are 'void makers'. Such situations challenge us to face the loss; to work with the emotions of the loss; and to accept the implications of the loss and the change that is needed in order to move on. If we do, the void then becomes a place that we remember but in a new light. It is no longer filled with dread. We shall have a sense of victory in place of the dread; we shall have conquered and defeated the dread, will have grown through the void. If we have been unable to face that place of loss, if we have not dealt with the inner pain, we may never be able to walk in confidence as we face the future. This book is about discovery, challenge, healing, and walking forward with new vision and understanding.

I hope that this book may be a useful resource to all who are hurting in some way and who are seeking answers to their inner pain; that it will be of interest and help to all and enable individuals to live life to the full, free from inner hurts that damage and cause them daily pain. This process of 'release' may well take time or it may come very quickly.

My physical healing was the start of a long journey for me: questions, seeking, growing, and the arrival at the discovery that my physical healing came from God. I needed to learn more about what the church offered. I began to learn about praying for healing, prayer ministry, and 'The Healing of the Family Tree' (see chapter 7). How, if at all, did they stand alongside the work of medical practitioners who offered healing to us? I studied theology and then, through my training as a counsellor, studied psychology. I began to see the whole. I could see a place for all ways of healing. It is rather like having a tool kit full of useful tools: not everyone needs every tool, but to have an overview of all the possibilities will ensure that the correct tools are used at the right time. I also came to see the importance of looking at the whole; that is to say, the body, the mind, and the spirit.

Loss through Physical Death

Many excellent books have been written about the loss of a loved one through death. This book is about other losses we may face in our lives, losses that also cause much grief and bereavement, so here we won't look specifically at loss due to the death of a loved one. It would be better to go to a book that specifically addresses this subject, which is significant for all of us. However, if you are in that place of grief, reading this book may trigger your thinking and help you to process the emotions that you may be experiencing.

The Task Ahead

We shall endeavour now to look at a range of situations that we come across in life where loss occurs. Having considered these situations, with new insights the reader may address the loss and change any area of hurt that may have resulted. Once that hurt has been understood and addressed, healing may be found for the hurt, the void. This is not a quick-fix job so be kind to yourself as you read. Remember that healing is a process; by reading this you have begun that process.

Chapter Two

Health Issues

An Overview and Consideration of Our Needs

To have good health is indeed a great blessing. It is often not until we are unable to continue our normal day-to-day activities as once we did due to some injury or illness or with the passing of years that we realise just how much we take our health for granted.

Take a young man in the peak of health. He is up at the front with the rest of his peer group in all physical activities. He then sustains a knee injury. Thinking it will heal, it comes as a great shock to him when he is told that it will not fully heal. He is no longer able to lead the field on the rugby pitch. For him, this will have a great impact upon his whole life. Suddenly, he is no long the leader of the pack. Once confident that he had the ability to get himself out of any situation, he is no longer able to do so. Over the years, it is possible that he will suffer frustration and his confidence may well decrease. How he views himself alongside his peers is all-important. His position will change. How he copes with his injury will be part of how he develops as an individual. It is not all gloom, but the situation will have an impact upon his life. It changes the scene for him.

The same is true for people who have physical illnesses that leave them not fully fit. They may still be able to do a great deal, and others around them may not even realise they suffer any difficulty. Those who look on may never know the struggle that is taking place within the individual in order to achieve what he or she does. Many struggle with pain, for instance. They may then also have to work with the side effects of medication that they need. Life will never be the same again. That is not to say it will not be good, but it will be different. As in the case of one who receives some physical injury, the way that person copes with illness of any sort will shape how he or she moves forward in life. In both instances, it is a loss. It will need some working through for each individual. The process may well involve anger, grief, frustration, and so on until there is an acceptance, and the person learns to live with the new self. This chapter will give just a few examples of life-changing situations that will challenge the individual within his or her physical body.

Loss may be seen as one grows older. The passage of years brings about changes; in the way we view ourselves, in the way others view us, in our physical and mental abilities. Changes may begin gradually, while others, like retirement or a health crisis, happen at a specific time. As the years go by, some say that they do not have the same energy, while others enter into retirement with increased energy and live life to the full, free from the constrains of daily paid work.

Growing older may be seen in terms of loss but also of gain. For some it brings a new sort of freedom. They no longer worry about how others see them. They are free to enjoy family in a new way. Becoming a grandparent may well open up a whole new chapter of life full of delight. It does so much depend upon where one lives and ones circumstances. Medical care, past ways of living, ones general health and ones lifestyle will all shape the way that we age.

Health issues are not just what may happen to our physical bodies. What about our mental state? How do our minds cope? For those of us who live in fast-moving, western societies, we are surrounded by new technology, new jargon, and new expectations. The twenty-first century may offer easy living for some but for others, the world seems really rather frightening.

Thanks to the microchip, we have all experienced great change in so many areas of our lives. Technology has certainly made great strides in a short space of time. It has opened up new horizons; we have so much on offer at the click of a mouse. Wonderful – but it has meant change, change, and more change.

For example, take how we once contacted a helpline. We dialled and usually spoke directly to a real person as the telephone was lifted up at the other end. I wonder how many of us now long to make contact with that person at the end of the telephone. We may, but only after a range of options given to us, initially offered by an automated voice. Having pressed an option or two, or even three, we then often have to listen to music that we may not like. We are then told that our call is very important. It may not feel like that to us. What message are we receiving as we hear those words? Far from feeling the call is important, we may begin to feel distinctly unimportant. No one, it seems, wants to hear us.

This emphasises the importance of being heard. To be heard is a crucial part of being us. We find ourselves in this fast-moving world and may feel very much not a part of it. We may then wonder what has replaced the old order. How does that make us feel?

For some, it may all begin to feel very unsafe, and we start to feel vulnerable. It may be that this sort of situation builds upon feelings of never being heard from years ago. Human interaction and respect one for another are both part of what we need day by day as individuals.

To continue this line of thinking, let us consider what we need to help us to feel safe and secure in our world. What are our needs beyond life-giving air, food, and water? We need love, security, discipline, work, and safe boundaries to know where we fit into society to live a life of significance and meaning so that we may reach our full potential.

Add in another need: the need of God or some higher force seems deeply embedded in our psyche. Many are grasping to find God in the new order of our world. Where is he in the chaos of bombs on buses and trains in London? Where is he in the plight of the hungry in Africa? The question of finding God in suffering seems all the more urgent for some.

This is not a textbook of psychological theories. However, a very brief overview of our basic needs will help to put the following chapters in context.

Physiological Needs

These are the need for oxygen, food and water, and a relatively constant body temperature. These are the first needs of an infant.

Safety Needs

Once our physiological needs have been met and are no longer the controlling thoughts and behaviours, the need for safety focuses our attention. As adults, living our daily lives, we may have little awareness of personal security needs. This soon changes when we move into a time of emergency (e.g. flooding or civil unrest) or into a time of disorganisation in the usual social structure (such as when there is a widespread terrorist alert in one of our cities).

It is, however, different for children, and they more readily tip over into displaying the signs of insecurity and the need to be safe. Observe the small child who suddenly cannot find Mummy in a supermarket. The world becomes a very scary place all at once. Back again with mother, everything feels so much better to the child.

Needs for Love and Belonging

When the needs for safety and for physiological well-being are satisfied, we then move onto the needs for love, affection, and belongingness. We seek to overcome feelings of loneliness and not being fully part of life by both giving and receiving love. We need to feel that we belong.

Need for Esteem

This may become a dominant need if the above needs have not been met in life. The problem of low self-esteem is seen as a reason for many difficult situations. We do best when we receive respect and also show respect to those around us. Humans have a need for a stable, firmly based, high level of self-respect.

With this by way of background, we now examine in more detail our needs for air, food and water, and a roof over our heads; the needs for love, security, discipline, the right occupation, safe boundaries and knowing where one fits into society; and the need to know God. And so back to looking at how we cope in body, mind and spirit. We may be fortunate and have thus far escaped any physical illness or injury. But how are we coping with life in our minds? And where, if at all, does the spirit come into our thinking?

I have selected a range of conditions I have encountered in my work. As you read, you might identify with some of the areas for yourself or for someone you know. The consistent health warning that goes with this book is: for all that I may identify symptoms regarding different types of conditions, it is crucial always to seek medical advice. Things are not always what they seem. My hope is that you will see the thinking behind the holistic approach.

Stress

The word stress is used often in our daily lives by both young and old. What do we mean by stress? Stress is caused by an existing stress-factor or what is called a "stressor." A stressor will come from the everyday activities or situations in our lives. Our physical, mental, or emotional adjustment or response to a stressful situation will make us feel 'stressed'.

However, what is stressful to one person is not necessarily stressful to another. The sort of factors that may cause stress will be life events like marriage, pregnancy, the birth of a child, a change in your financial situation, a change in your health or that of a family member, a change of school, a new job, the death of a loved one, difficulty at work, redundancy and so on; some things might appear quite minor, like finding the way out of a strange building or rushing to catch a bus. When we find ourselves in a stressful situation, the brain signals a chemical release to help us deal with it. These chemical substances trigger a series of responses that give the body extra energy to cope appropriately.

Stress is a normal part of life and in small quantities is good. It can motivate you and can help you to be more productive. However, too much stress – or an excessive response to stress – is harmful as it may cause distress and lead to health problems. To find the right balance for us, we need to learn how our bodies respond to the demands of daily life. If every day seems stressful to you, then you may need to consider how you may find a better balance for yourself. So just because those around you can cope, it does not mean that you can or should. If you are able to recognise the early signs of stress and then do something about them, you may make an important difference to the quality of your life.

Do you feel under stress? Below is a list of some of the signals that may indicate stress. It is most important that you do not make your own diagnosis, as signals in the body may indicate another condition. Only a medical practitioner should make a diagnosis.

- General irritability
- The overpowering urge to cry, or run and hide
- Inability to concentrate, flight of thoughts, and general disorientation
- Easily tired; loss of "joie de vivre" (the joy of life)
- "Floating anxiety", a generalized sense of apprehension without a focus
- Emotional tension or a feeling of being "keyed up"
- Insomnia
- Loss of appetite or compulsive eating

If you work in a high-pressure environment, it is essential to have times of rest and relaxation. If this is not possible, the danger is that the demands will exceed your coping skills. Your ability to handle stress then deteriorates. What happens next will vary, but there will be some sort of toll on your body or mind. Think of the effect upon a car driving at high speeds for long periods of time. With no pit stops for care and maintenance to be given, the engine will burn out. Trying to handle too much all of the time is a human equivalent. Our bodies need times of rest – time to relax – so that we are then able to get back to work. If you seem unable to take hold of the situation, do talk to someone who can help you to defuse it and thus enable you to take stock.

Panic Attacks

Related perhaps to stress, is the panic attack. Real and intense to the individual going through such an experience, a panic attack may be described as a time of great fear or discomfort.

Below are listed just some of the symptoms. You may have experienced some of them if indeed you have had a panic attack. Please do note that these symptoms may indicate other problems. This is why it is so important that you consult your doctor in order that a correct diagnosis may be made.

- Pounding heart or accelerated heart rate
- Sweating, trembling or shaking sensations
- Shortness of breath, feelings of choking
- Nausea
- Feeling dizzy

A panic attack may be so disabling that the individual is unable to express to others what is happening to them. The person may appear terrified or shaky or be hyperventilating (deep, rapid breathing which may cause dizziness).

People have spoken to me about their panic attacks. They can last all day or for a short period. Once in the attack, the individuals talk about being 'frozen' by the fear, unable to make any decisions, and unable to operate in a normal manner. They may need to pace the floor, quite unable to sit still.

If you do have panic attacks, or what you believe to be a panic attack, you should see your doctor and talk it through with him or her. You will be guided by them as to the reason why you feel as you do. It is best to deal with it and to find the root cause. Counselling may well be helpful after you have seen your doctor.

Depression

Depression has been termed 'the common cold of mental health'. Many people feel 'down', or 'blue', from time to time; that is not uncommon. But when does feeling 'down' cross the line into depression? If you feel that you are stuck in a state of depression and the feelings just do not lift, do seek medical help. The reasons for depression are complex, but there is a great deal of understanding and help available.

As you read this, if you feel depressed, you may think that you know the cause; it may be clear to you. However, the reasons for depression may not be clear;

that is, there may not be just one cause, but a variety of contributing factors that accumulate over time and lead to the feeling of hopelessness, of being defeated, demoralized, and helpless, and thus depressed. And sometimes, with factors like low self-esteem or anxiety, it may be almost impossible to say which causes which. It is these many possibilities that make the condition of depression so complex.

Common Symptoms of Depression

- Physical: changes in sleep pattern; changes in eating patterns; fatigue, loss of energy
- Behavioural: diminished interest in, and enjoyment of, previously pleasurable activities; difficulty in concentrating or making decisions
- Emotional: depressed mood (can mean feeling down, apathetic, irritable, pessimistic, hopeless, helpless, negative, guilty, anxious, empty, and so forth); feelings of worthlessness

What Can You Do About It?

There are actually a lot of things you can do about depression but you do need to talk it through with your doctor. Often a combination of medical help and counselling is most helpful. Some counsellors think that if an individual is on medication, they are not able to enter into counselling. That is not my experience. Someone who is deeply depressed will find it difficult to work in the counselling setting. If they will be guided by their doctor and start on medication, this should reduce pressure on the individual and alleviate their symptoms and then the counselling is usually very helpful. They can then begin more comfortably to look at the reasons behind the depression.

Depression can leave you feeling helpless and out of control of your life, your thoughts, feelings, and behaviours. You want to regain and experience more power and control; you want to get to the point where you feel as though you can do something to improve your situation and life.

Bipolar Disorder

Bipolar disorder, also known as manic-depressive illness, is a brain disorder that causes unusual shifts in a person's mood, energy, and ability to function. Different from the normal ups and downs that everyone goes through, the symptoms of bipolar disorder are severe. The result of such mood swings leads to great difficulties – damaged relationships and problems in one's working world to name but two areas. Those who have this condition suffer, and those around them also suffer as they watch and wait for mood swings. But there is good news: bipolar disorder can be treated and people with this illness can lead full and productive lives. However, an added complication arises if there are problems in the individual's background. This is where counselling can be most helpful, but it is important to find the right time for the individual according to where they are in their cycle of illness.

Attention Deficit Hyperactivity Disorder (ADHD) and Attention Deficit Disorder (ADD)

These problems refer to a range of behaviours associated with poor attention span found in both adults and children. They may include impulsiveness, restlessness, and hyperactivity, as well as inattentiveness. The child will often have difficulty in their learning as well as their socialising.

Children with this condition clearly need to have had a detailed medical assessment. The sort of symptoms to look out for will be the child's apparent inability to finish tasks or sustain attention in play activities. They may seem not to listen and so fail to follow instructions they are given. They are often disorganised, never seem to have their hands on what is needed for the task (e.g. pencils and books). And they are easily distracted, and forgetful in the course of daily activities.

In terms of their hyperactivity, they run around excessively often wanting to climb, are unduly noisy in playing, and have difficulty in engaging in quiet leisure activities. The child will find it difficult to sit still in the classroom, and there may be a great deal of fidgeting and shuffling of hands and feet. They may come out with answers before the question is completed. They may find it difficult to wait in lines or to wait for their turn in games or group situations. They may interrupt other children's conversations or games.

There are other difficulties that can occur alongside ADHD. Children may exhibit temper tantrums, sleep disorders, and display confrontational, defiant behaviour.

Now, please, do not jump to the wrong conclusions. Many children may be very active or be easily distracted or have difficulty concentrating. If these behaviours are relatively mild, they should not be considered a disorder. However, about 1.7 per cent of the UK population, mostly children, have ADD or ADHD, and boys are more likely to be affected.

The above is a very cursory look at ADHD and ADD; quite clearly, the individual will need a correct medical assessment. The condition requires a diagnosis by a doctor: usually a child or adolescent psychiatrist, a paediatrician or paediatric neurologist. It will often be appropriate for other professionals such as psychologists, speech therapists, teachers and health visitors, to contribute their observations to the assessment of a child with possible ADHD or ADD. There is no single diagnostic test for these conditions, so different sorts of information need to be gathered together.

Treatment depends on a child's exact diagnosis. Management techniques for parents and teachers (such as creating a daily routine for the child, giving clear instructions and reasonable requests, the setting of clear and easily understood boundaries, and being consistent in the handling and managing of the child) have all proved to be helpful.

Alongside behavioural management techniques medication may be offered. This, of course, would all be discussed with the doctor. Children may also receive help with social and communication skills.

Autism

Autism is often described as a 'spectrum disorder' because the condition affects people in many different ways and to varying degrees. People with autism have described their world as a mass of people, places, and events all of which they struggle to make sense of, and which can cause them considerable anxiety.

In particular, understanding and relating to other people and taking part in everyday family and social life may be harder for them. The ability to know, intuitively, how to communicate and interact with others is a skill not to be taken for granted for people with this problem.

We may not be aware of it, but when we meet a person, we sum them up from their facial expression, tone of voice, and body language. We are usually able to tell whether they are happy, angry, or sad. This being so, we may respond accordingly.

A problem for those with autism is that they may find it more difficult to read the signals that most of us take for granted. This means that they find it more difficult to communicate and interact with others. This can then lead to high levels of anxiety and confusion.

Asperger's Syndrome is a form of autism that affects how a person makes sense of the world, processes information, and relates to other people. It is mostly a 'hidden disability', meaning that, from an outward appearance, one cannot tell that someone has Asperger's Syndrome. Their condition affects three main areas in their lives and makes for difficulties with social communication, social interaction, and social imagination. They, therefore, can have problems when it comes to relationships.

Dyslexia

The word 'dyslexia' comes from the Greek and means 'difficulty with words'. Dyslexia is a specific disability that mainly affects the development of literacy and language-related skills. It is likely to be present at birth and to have lifelong effects, and tends to be resistant to conventional teaching methods. Fortunately, there is a far greater understanding of the condition now, and new teaching methods are used to good effect. Many who suffer from dyslexia are of high intelligence, and their condition may cause them great frustration, but it can also result in an ability to work round and through the difficulties.

Obsessive-Compulsive Disorder (OCD)

For those who suffer from OCD, the intensity of the condition will vary. Some who experience this condition describe recurrent and persistent thoughts, impulses, or images that are experienced, at some time during the disturbance, as intrusive, inappropriate, and causing marked anxiety or distress.

The compulsion part comes through as repetitive behaviours (e.g., hand washing, checking, following a specific pattern for activities, counting, repeating words silently), which the person feels driven to perform in response to their obsession.

The obsessions or compulsions can cause marked distress, are time-consuming, and can significantly interfere with the person's normal routine, occupational (or academic) functioning, or usual social activities or relationships.

CASE STUDY: Lily

Lily started to see me because of an eating disorder. She had received much help, but nothing seemed to be effective. She suffered from Anorexia Nervosa – I touch on eating disorders later in this chapter – and had developed OCD. This took the form of excessive hand washing and checking. Lily was almost a prisoner in her own home. To ensure that she was safe at home, she had developed a routine that demanded certain rituals in each room of the house. Light switches, plugs, lights, electrical equipment, windows, cupboard doors, and so on, all had to be checked and re-checked again and again. The routine for each room took up to thirty minutes. Once completed, the door was shut. This routine started every morning. By lunchtime, she had completed the routine and ended up captive in one room. If she opened a door of a checked room, then she was 'unsafe', and the routine had to start all over again. Getting out of the house was difficult to say the least, as she had to start early in the morning if she needed to be anywhere by midmorning. It was very sad and distressing for her.

Post-Traumatic Stress Disorder (PTSD)

PTSD can start after any traumatic event. A traumatic event may be defined as an event where we can see that we are in danger, our life is threatened, or where we see other people dying or being injured. On the news, we frequently hear of soldiers returning from the front line and how they may suffer from PTSD.

Possible 'trigger points' for setting this condition off would be serious road accidents, military combat, violent personal assault (sexual assault, physical attack, abuse, robbery, or mugging), being taken hostage, terrorist attack, being a prisoner-of-war, and natural or man-made disasters. This is not to say that everyone experiencing such events will suffer from this condition, but they may.

The symptoms of PTSD usually start some time after the event. It can be several weeks or even months. They usually appear within six months but not in all cases. An individual may experience something traumatic and hold it all within until something else 'triggers' the past memories. This is then very difficult, as the original event has been pushed down and becomes all mixed up with the trigger point which may, on the surface, seem quite a minor or non-event.

Feelings experienced by those who have this condition will vary. Individuals may have a cloud of grief over them. They may feel low and anxious, or guilty and angry. They may not be able to voice why they feel as they feel or, indeed, quite what they feel. Alongside the emotions, there will be a range of symptoms.

Often talked about are flashbacks and nightmares. The cause becomes evident if they have specific flashbacks or nightmares about or relating to the event. Ordinary things can trigger flashbacks. For example, if you were in a train accident, hearing the noise of a train can cause a flashback. You may then develop avoidance behaviour. You will go out of your way to avoid being near any situation that may remind you of the trauma. Some people will become emotionally numb and retreat into their own world to stay safe.

Being 'on guard' may well be a feature. You stay alert all the time, as if you are looking out for danger. You can't relax. This is called 'hypervigilance'. Sleep may be difficult. Others will notice that you are jumpy, irritable, anxious, or deeply withdrawn. There may be other symptoms that will confuse the root of the problem. Together with the emotional reactions, the sufferer may experience such things as muscle aches and pains, headaches, feelings of panic and fear, and depression. They may also use drink and drugs to numb the emotional pain.

It is important to note that certainly not everyone will experience PTSD after a traumatic experience. However, many will have the symptoms of post-traumatic stress for the first month or so. This is because they help to keep you going; they help you to understand and so process the experience you have been through. Over a few weeks, most people slowly come to terms with what has happened, and their stress symptoms start to disappear. If there were other people with you when the trauma took place, talking through the experience together will help a great deal.

For some, their symptoms do not leave them; the process has got stuck. The symptoms of post-traumatic stress, although normal in themselves, become a problem and may in turn develop into post-traumatic stress disorder (PTSD).

Clearly, professional help is needed at this stage. There is a range of treatments including different forms of therapy. Talking, painting, and writing about the experience – to name but a few lines of therapy – all help to get it out into the open in order to take away the hold and fear that has become embedded.

Schizophrenia

This is a distressing illness, and the sufferer needs help. The person concerned will need to be under the care of a psychiatrist. Symptoms vary to a great degree but may include delusions, phobias, hallucinations, and confused thinking. Some people may experience only one or more brief episodes, while for others schizophrenia remains a lifelong condition. A great deal can be done to help with the correct treatment. One of the problems is ensuring that the person who suffers takes the correct medication; this is very important indeed. The temptation to cease taking it is not uncommon. Should this occur those who live alongside – or have care for – the individual will have to field a change in behaviour and potentially distressing emotional outbursts. It can feel like a rollercoaster of ups and downs that are repeated until some sort of stability via medication can be established.

Personality Disorders

There can be great confusion when one starts to discuss personality disorders. They are complex and can only be diagnosed by professionals. We are talking here about a general term for a type of mental illness in which ways of thinking, perceiving situations, and relating to others will be different from those considered to be in the normal range.

There are many specific types of personality disorders. Some types of disorder lead to clear distress within the individual. However in some cases, the individual may not realise that they have a personality disorder. This is because their way of thinking and behaving seems natural to them. It is not a problem to them although it may be a problem for those around them. I shall mention just a few out of the great range of personality disorders. I have chosen ones that some of you may have come across and ones that have come my way in the counselling room.

Borderline Personality Disorder (BPD)

This is seen in young people as well as in those in later life. This condition affects how you feel about yourself, how you relate to others, and how you behave. Those with BPD often have an insecure sense of who they are and where they belong. They seem unsure as to where and how they fit into life. One person described how they felt by saying that they "did not feel comfortable in their own skin".

This illness interferes with an individual's ability to regulate emotion and this emotional instability will result in shifts of mood. The person may seem to be detached from those around them, finding it most difficult to communicate and share feelings and emotions. When they do feel emotions, these can come out with great force leaving the receiver of their outburst perplexed and possibly frightened. Symptoms range greatly and some people with BPD will live and work quite satisfactorily on the face of it for many years. However, events or relationships will trigger outbursts. The individual needs routine as well as little or no emotional challenge. This makes the possibility of close emotional relationships seem almost unattainable.

For some, the illness may become apparent in teenage years. For others, it comes in adulthood perhaps triggered by some trauma such as the death of a parent or some life change that puts pressure upon the individual. Life just gets to be too much.

For a young person the diagnosis will probably come after many distressing and possibly life-endangering events. Wanting to be like their friends, they may find themselves at university unable to cope with the demands both socially and at work. I have seen the pain and sense of failure in young people who seem to fall by the wayside (in some cases literally) with uncontrolled drinking and a terror of life out of control. They have eventually had medical intervention and BPD has been diagnosed. The chances are that the young person will have had a very rough ride up to that point with recriminations and disapproval from those around them.

Relationships are very difficult for individuals with BPD. To give and receive emotionally in a way that is acceptable to the other half of the relationship will prove most difficult. To communicate in an emotional way is not easy and may well become impossible. It is not uncommon for anger and frustration, felt within the one who suffers with this disorder, to be displayed in inappropriate ways. Behaviour may include out-of-character ways such as free and fluid sexual relationships outside the marriage (if they are within such a relationship), being tempted and perhaps being drawn into pornography or other 'risky' sexual areas that they would deny if questioned. They easily become addicted to everyday things in life such as alcohol, betting, web-searching, and television. For some the only safe way is to very firmly avoid such areas.

If the diagnosis of BPD is made when someone is in a relationship, the partner will experience pain and shock as events of the past unravel. It may be seen that out-of-character behaviour had been present but the balance was more towards the 'norm' and, as a result, unusual events had been ignored. Even when a diagnosis has been made (normally by two medical practitioners in the field of psychology), the partner may well find it hard to accept until the behaviour becomes more extreme and out of character.

Such situations are extremely difficult for those who have a family because not only the partner but also the children and potentially the extended family will be caught up in this illness. The one who is ill seldom can see their unreasonable and deeply hurtful behaviour. They therefore do not usually receive any ongoing therapeutic help, as they see no need for it. Indeed, if such help is given it is not unusual for them to play the system and appear to triumph over those who seek to help them.

Below is a case of an individual who clearly battled with BPD from a young age. The pain for the parents and siblings is great in such cases, just as it is for those in a relationship with someone who displays the behaviour at a later stage in their life.

CASE STUDY: Joan

Joan came to me as a young adult. She was a high achiever and had gone off to university. It was at university that her problems came to the fore. Unable to find the balance between work and play, she slipped into a highly charged social life with much drinking. The work side really never took off. Joan left university after the first year.

She talked about her unstable relationships and impulsive behaviour. She had felt very left out at university, drinking the night away, and then waking up to no friends. This left her with a fear of being left alone. She had started to cling on to anyone who would have her. This need for dependency led her to several very unsatisfactory sexual relationships. She had very low self-esteem and therefore was unsure of her own identity.

She had also begun to act impulsively in ways that were self-damaging, with much spending of money, binge eating, and little care for herself. She had started to have recurring suicidal thoughts and had made one attempt before she came to me. She had also started to cut herself to 'take away the pain'. This was a form of self-harm.

Joan experienced mood swings, including feeling depressed, irritable, or anxious. She talked about feeling empty inside. She was clearly taking little responsibility for her well-being.

Joan and I worked together for some months. She was clearly a very distressed young woman. She needed very much more help than I could give; eventually, Joan was diagnosed with BPD. The diagnosis quite shocked her, yet it also gave her and her family something upon which to measure the difficulties. Joan received a range of treatments including a six-month residential programme. Helpful to her was the skills-based approach, which looked at how to regulate her emotions, tolerate distress, and improve relationships. Also helpful was medication to help the anxiety. Part of what I was able to do was to help and to encourage her parents to seek further help for Joan. It was a case of one step at a time in a multi-faceted situation.

The stigma of having a mental health difficulty, illness, or disorder can often leave a person frightened to talk about their problem and reluctant to access support. Understanding the mental health system, the function of counsellors, therapists, psychotherapists, psychologists and psychiatrists, and the different treatment approaches may feel very frightening. As a counsellor, I see many distressed individuals of all ages who suffer to some degree with mental disorders.

Bullying

Bullying can happen to anyone at any age. Being bullied may take place in any setting; at home, at school, in the work place, in social settings, on line and via other communication systems like mobile phones. It may take some of the following forms; being physically hit, being teased, called names, been threatened with words, having false rumours spread about you, being ignored and left out, being threatened or intimidated, even looks may be a way to bully another.

Bullying is persistent unwelcome behaviour in whatever setting. Anyone who chooses to bully is admitting their inadequacy. Bullies project their inadequacy onto others by; avoiding having to face their own inadequacy, to avoid accepting responsibility for their behaviour and the effect it has on others, to reduce their fear of being seen for what they are – weak and inadequate and often incompetent individuals. Their behaviour diverts attention from their shortcomings.

Bullying may leave long lasting results; stress and

depression, anxiety, low self-esteem, hopelessness, helplessness and isolation both in children and later in life as adults. Some adults still recalled bullying incidents from thirty or more years ago. Being a person who is present when another is bullied has an effect on the bystander too. They feel compromised, helpless and guilty

Self Harm

Self-harm may embrace any action that harms ones body but specifically will take the form of taking tablets; cutting, burning, piercing or swallowing objects. Some people self-harm regularly - it can become almost an addiction. The reasons for self-harm will vary. An individual who self-harms will often be in a state of high emotion and inner turmoil. This may be caused by abuse; feeling depressed; feeling bad about themselves or they may have relationship problems. The individual may feel unheard, unloved, isolated, alone and out of control. Those who do self-harm report that it helps them to feel more in control and less tense. So, it can be a 'quick fix' for feeling bad. It is an action that will need to be repeated, as it is not a long-term solution to the problem. Under the heading of self harm we now move onto Eating Disorders – an action of self harm.

Eating Disorders

Eating disorders cause much distress to the one who suffers and to those around them. An eating disorder is to eat, or avoid eating, in a way which negatively affects both one's physical and mental health. Eating disorders are all encompassing. They affect every part of the person's life. Listed below are details of the most common eating disorders with possible effects. Please do note that not everyone will experience the whole range listed and indeed may develop other problems. This is therefore only a guide.

Anorexia Nervosa

This is the relentless pursuit of thinness through self-starvation. Anorexia is a potentially life threatening psychological disorder. People with anorexia have a huge fear of normal body weight and feel fat, even when they are at a dangerously low weight.

Physical effects

Constantly cold, dry skin and hair, periods stop, difficulty sleeping, bones jut out, muscles weaken, brittle bones, stomach pains, low blood pressure, constipation, feeling of dizziness, depression, slowness of thought and possible effect on vital organs.

Psychological effects

Obsessed with food, isolated from others, negativity, extreme fear of weight gain, panic attacks, mood swings, obsessive behaviour, secrecy, hyperactivity.

What to look out for

Personality changes and withdrawal from friendships, tendency to perfectionism, moodiness, weight loss when already very slim, baggy clothes, avoidance of food/meals with the family, reluctance to eat in front of others, a rigid inflexible regime.

Who is affected by anorexia?

Found in men and women of all ages and from all social and ethnic groups, but the largest number of diagnosed cases is among young women in their teens.

Research has shown that those with obsessive or perfectionist personalities, combined with other difficulties in their lives, are the most susceptible to developing anorexia.

Bulimia Nervosa

Recurrent bouts of binge eating, followed by self-induced vomiting, laxative or diuretic abuse followed by long periods of fasting forming a continuous cycle.

Physical effects

Stomach pains, sore throat, dehydration, mouth infections, tooth decay, kidney damage, irregular periods, swollen glands, hair loss, bloodshot eyes, rapid weight fluctuations, dry skin.

Psychological effects

Shame and guilt, obsessed with food and weight, distancing self from reality, anxiety, irrational behaviour, avoid eating with others.

What to look out for

Leaving room immediately after meals, large consumption of fluid during meals, large amounts of food disappearing, weight fluctuations, depression, mood swings.

Who is affected by Bulimia

Anyone, but it is most commonly seen in women in their late teens and early twenties.

Harder to spot than anorexia as weight is usually within the normal range.

Binge-Eating Disorder

Recurrent episodes of binge-eating with feelings of loss of control.

Physical effects

Feeling bloated, lethargic, rapid weight gain, risk of heart disease, possible high blood pressure.

Psychological effects

Obsessed with food, feel emotionally empty, guilt and self-disgust, feel unable to control the amount of food eaten.

What to look for

Often eating much faster that usual, eating in privacy, eating when not hungry, eating to relieve stress and to avoid social functions.

Who is affected by Binge-Eating Disorder

Most sufferers are obese and it is slightly more common in females than males.

Research shows that up to half of the sufferers also suffer from depression.

Range of Possible Treatments

Go to G.P.

Referral to a specialist for further assessment

Outpatient treatment

Hospital stay

Residential care

Counselling. A list of specialist counsellors may be found on the beat or the ABC website listed at the end of this chapter.

CASE STUDY: As spoken by a 15 year-old anorexia sufferer

How am I? What do I feel?

You become obsessed with doing everything possible to burn calories.

Every spare minute is used to exercise.

Your mind becomes totally occupied with calculating how many calories everything contains, and also how you can avoid any meals.

You become very deceitful.

You start to lose interest in your friends and withdraw.

You feel uncomfortable in a large group because you think that everyone else just sees you as a body and, what's more, a fat body!

So you stop going out at all and just stay at home, exercising or studying.

I must get all A grades in my exams.

You cause your family a tremendous amount of pain. My parents feel that they've failed; I hear them having rows. My Dad shouts out that Mum never has time for him now. I feel really bad, yet also a little smug. I am the focus of my Mum's attention.

I want my Mum. I don't want to grow up. My younger sister has become very resentful towards me.

She does not understand why I'm committing a slow suicide.

I am always so cold.

It becomes painful to sit for too long or to sit on a hard chair.

I want to hide my body.

When I had to go away for treatment I missed so much schoolwork.

I hated it first of all in hospital, but I really felt like I had won. I was a really good anorexic. I always want to be the best, and I had achieved the best as I lay there.

It was not so good when I was then sent away. I hated being with others who could not eat. That made me the same. I want to be unique. This is my special problem.

I've lost virtually all of my friends.

Now I have started to cut my arms. It is a different sort of pain. But I really must keep this a big secret. No one must know about this. What if I get an infection? I don't care. Or do I?

I don't know what I want anymore.

Maybe try to throw up again. I don't like to vomit, but I have found out how to do it.

I hide that well from Mum. I know all about my teeth. I know, I know

Do I want to get better? No. Well, that is what I think now. Maybe someone can help me to feel better.

I have so much stuff in my mind. How can I get to it and find me again?

Who am I now?

One can hear the fear and confusion and wrong thinking in the mind of that young lady.

The whole area of mental illness is complex. There are no neat answers and there is much overlap. The range of drugs to help is great, but the right drug needs to be found for each individual. While I always encourage people to seek medical help, it is then a case of discovering the root cause of their illness. Events from the past will almost certainly have influenced the condition. Indeed, in some instances, events past and present may well have actually triggered the condition.

Once the individual's condition is a little improved, then is the time to consider such trigger points.

With the right help, great insights may be found, and the cycle of distress that has caused the illness may be addressed. There are no promises in this statement, but to seek out a counsellor who is equipped to work with and explore things with you will reveal the areas in your life that were the origin of this illness. Counselling takes work and commitment from the individual. In areas such as depression, the results can be most significant. Again and again, I have seen people 'freed up' and doctors remarking that the drugs seem to have acted very fast. The drugs have helped that person to be in a place where, in safety, they can dare to look at past issues. Then the real healing comes.

Our minds are complex. We 'inform' and shape them as we go through life, and trauma can take a big toll upon them. While it is always right to seek help from the medical profession, we can also seek help in the form of counselling. This is the inner healing bit: unlocking the past in a safe way to be able then to seek discernment. An area that is dark and muddled needs light shed upon it. With care we unfold the past, and the light comes into the dark places. Darkness often indicates fear. Shedding light into the darkness starts the process of release. Medication and therapy go hand in hand in this way.

Some people are looking for a complete cure. With things of the mind, I have had to learn that in some cases it is about learning to live with the new you.

Anyone who has had a breakdown and recovered from one of these conditions will, I think, know what I mean. The person gets better but is changed; that change may well be for the good, but it is a new you. You are more sensitive, more cautious, wiser, and so on. While drug treatment may well be crucial, it does not always seem to be the whole answer. It is about finding out the triggers that cause the inner distress and, if possible, dealing with them. That makes it sound very simple. It is not. It is very challenging for all concerned.

I am not considering here the problems presented through the misuse of drugs and drink. This is a complex area that needs therapeutic help specifically geared to the situation. I do, however, work with parents who suffer from watching their children fall into these areas of addiction. It is so very painful for them.

Another Look at Physical Illness

We can all too easily take good health for granted. It is a shock when something goes wrong with the body. In so many cases, thanks to medical science, we may be helped to recover. But for some, at any age, chronic illness sets in and becomes part of our lives. It is a shock, and we have to start to journey on the unfamiliar territory of hospitals, doctors, tests, and waiting.

Being ill takes control away from the individual. They need to learn to remain very positive as they do all that they can to get back to health. They find themselves in 'the system', which often means an endless round of doctors and investigations.

Step into a rehabilitation unit and talk to the patients. You will find differing attitudes, of course, but in the main the patients have a determination to get well. They find a fight within them and, helped along by professionals, other patients and family and friends, they dig deep into their inner reserves and find the courage and strength to begin to heal. Rehabilitation is the end process that some find themselves in after an illness, accident, or stroke, which has left the body weak and unable to function as it once did. Rehabilitation is about helping the person to get their physical body back to being as whole as possible, and being helped mentally and emotionally during the process. It is about their acceptance of the 'new person they have become'.

CASE STUDY: John

John was a man in his early fifties who had suffered a stroke. When I met him, he was in his hospital bed looking downcast while his wife sat by him holding his hand. John had lost the use of his leg, arm, and hand on one side of his body. He'd enjoyed living an active life until this blow came upon him.

Over the weeks, which then stretched into months, I watched and listened to John as he found strength to rebuild his body. After the initial shock, he had started the long haul back. He was determined to rebuild his body. There were tears and frustrations and grey days. On such days, his fellow patients seemed to rally round him. There was a certain humour between them that goaded them on and forward.

In moments of quiet, John did a great deal of thinking. In between the activity were times of boredom. His mind was good. It was his body that prevented him from doing all the things that he once did. It became a battle of mind and body; spirit also came into his thinking. Life-changing events do have a way of focusing the mind. I watched John grow as a person. He left the hospital a changed man; changed, he said, for the better. Such an experience makes or breaks a person.

So how has it been for you?

Have you been through physical or mental illness? How has it left you? What loss have you experienced, and how have you found living with the 'new you'? Have you watched a close family member battle with illness? Has it left you with unresolved issues? Do you live with a partner who is not as he or she once was? Are you left with fears or memories that you would prefer not to remain in your mind?

We are resilient but do have our limit. That limit will be different for each of us. We need to know our limit and live life accordingly. Is there discomfort that in some way invades your everyday life? It is possible to work on such issues. Some people think that they should be able to manage on their own with whatever they have been through. This is not so. We vary in our ability to cope with situations, and the timing of such situations is also a factor.

Remember back to the death of Diana, Princess of

Wales. There was a display of national grief – not at all typically 'British', but somehow her death triggered off the emotions of the nation. Of course, there was heartfelt agony and grief over her death; it was the most appalling loss. However, her death also triggered off a well of emotions that were stored deep within the hearts of the British people.

Emotions

Emotions are strong within us. As we begin to feel something, we may block those feelings; we put up our defence walls. If we go with the feelings – sadness perhaps – that sad feeling, that emotion, will sweep over us. We may cry, or we may simply hold in the sadness. If no tears are forthcoming, an observant person may yet see that sadness in our faces.

Expressing your emotions may be something that you do often or you may, for whatever reason, hold back on the expression. You may sense that it is not safe to let the feeling take you along. Our ability to feel and express our emotions may in part be due to our background. As a child, did you express how you felt? Were you allowed to do so? Do you share your feelings with others now? How comfortable are you with touch? Do you feel embarrassed when there is a show of emotion from others? How do you feel when someone starts to cry? Do you want to stop them? Or walk away? Or do you instinctively want to comfort them and stay with them in their emotion? How you respond to these questions may give you insight as to how you relate to others and to how you express your own emotions.

Below are some helplines and sources of information.

Depression and Bipolar support group go to: http://www.dbsalliance.org/

Mind; mental health issues: http://www.mind.org.uk/

Eating Disorders

Anorexia and Bulimia Care - Tel. 01934 713789

ABC is a Christian charity working to support all who suffer because of eating disorders

mail@anorexiabulimiacare.co.uk

www.anorexiabulimiacare.co.uk

Parents' helpline: 01934 710645

Sufferers helpline: 01934 710679

beat - National Eating Disorders Association)

beat - Helpline 0845 634 1414 help@b-eat.co.uk

beat - Youth line 0845 634 7650 fyp@b-eat.co.uk

Childline – 0800 1111 wwwChildLine.org.uk

Free and confidential helpline for children and young adults.

Bullying in the workplace

- http://www.nationalbullyinghelpline.co.uk

Beat Bullying - www.beatbullying.co.uk

Chapter Three

Criminal Actions

Crime affects people in many different ways. It may come as a surprise just how emotional someone feels after being a victim of crime. Strong emotions may rise up within them. Such emotions can make one feel even more unsettled and confused. Those around someone who has suffered criminal action, such as partners, children, and friends, will also be affected. Crime has that sort of ripple effect. Those caught up in this ripple may feel similar emotions to yours, as well as concern for you.

Victims of crime need to express and explore their reactions. They experience new and strong emotions, yet so often they find that those around them expect them to 'get over it'. This is not very helpful if what they need to do is to talk and work out why they feel as they do.

Some factors that will determine how you might react to crime

- The type of crime
- Whether you knew the person who committed the crime
- The kind of support you received from the police, your family, and friends
- If you have other support, such as counselling
- Past hurtful events that you have experienced. Do they have any impact on how you feel now?

The effects of crime can last for a very long time. Your reaction may not correspond with the severity of the crime. Others may think the event was minor, yet you may have a severe reaction.

If you find yourself unable to recover after such an unwanted intrusion into your life, do seek further help. Without such help, you may develop long-term problems such as depression or an anxiety-related illness. Some people experience post-traumatic stress disorder. This is a medical term used to describe a pattern of symptoms found in a person who has experienced some sort of traumatic event. One factor that may make coping with crime especially hard is if it was personalized; that is, if the crime was directly and deliberately aimed at you personally.

People who commit crime do so with the intent to cause harm. If you are the victim, this can make you feel powerless and vulnerable. This is especially difficult to deal with if the crime is repeated or ongoing, which is often the case with domestic violence or abuse.

Up to two and a half million people are assaulted or threatened every year. Threats and verbal abuse are forms of violence just as much as physical attacks. These violent crimes can take place anywhere: at home, in the street, in the car, at work, in clubs, and in pubs. Violent crime can be a very frightening experience. Quite new emotions are stirred within, and there is often a fear that such an attack will happen again.

We now look at some actions that are of a criminal nature. It is obvious that some are just that (i.e. criminal). Some areas may not seem so clear but, nonetheless, they are criminal. The very fact that we accept that they are, indeed, criminal proves helpful because by this we acknowledge the pain that they cause to the victims.

Looking at Robbery

By definition, robbery is when something is taken from you with violence or threats. It is a violent act even if you are not physically hurt. It is a frightening experience, especially if a weapon is used. It may be directly aimed at you – when it is a direct attack upon your person in order to get something of value from you – or indirectly, as in the case of house burglary. Depending when you happen upon the burglary, you will still feel that it is a personal violation because your own space has been invaded and your privacy violated.

CASE STUDY: Two Couples

In a certain country several years ago, two couples drove back to their home. They had security gates that opened and closed on a timer. As they climbed out of the car, three men jumped at them brandishing guns. They demanded money and the keys for the car.

One of the men involved kept a very cool head. At that point, it became a game of nerves. In a low voice, he told the woman to move slowly to his rear. He stood up tall and calmly offered the keys of his car and emptied the contents of his pockets. He said it all felt like slow motion until his friend moved to the side of him, and at that point he heard a loud crack. A gun had been fired. The man next to him crumpled. It would have been normal to rush to help the wounded man, but instead he offered his watch. He took the focus back to himself. He slowly gestured the attackers into the car and pointed out that the electric gates would soon close, indicating that they needed to go but without telling them to do so. Still standing tall, he watched the men drive off in the car just before the gates closed on a remote timer.

The incident was bad enough, but it could have been so much worse. His bravery meant that the women literally faded into the shadows. They were neither an irritant nor a temptation. Their raw fear was unseen and therefore did not aggravate the situation. Quite why the men fired when they did is not known, but it may be because the focus was on the man who was talking and that the movement of the second man unnerved them.

All four were left in shock. Fortunately the man who was fired upon received a flesh wound that healed up well. The man who had become the chief spokesperson had encountered other violent situations and was able to hold his nerve and keep his calm. They were able to talk to each other about the experience, which was helpful. Fear could have taken a long-lasting grip upon them, but they dealt with the experience and resolved not to be victims forever.

Those who have been together as victims in any one incident are helped by talking to one another because they have a shared experience. Some people find it helpful to talk to someone outside the situation. This is a way of 'off loading' the memory and lessening the impact of the experience.

House burglary

Talk to anyone whose home has been burgled. They can 'feel' the people who invaded their space. It leaves a horrid feeling and takes a great deal of courage and 'working at' to create that safe space within their home again. Some will wash all the areas that they feel hands may have touched; some will re-decorate the rooms that were invaded; further security systems will be put into place, and a level of anxiety will remain for some time to come. As also for victims of other criminal actions, there is a need for victims of a house burglary to talk about the experience.

Potential Criminal Action

Even if no crime is actually committed, one may be left feeling vulnerable for years to come if there is a near encounter.

CASE STUDY: Sue and Claire

These two young girls were walking along a street in an East African town. They had some cash on them and both wore watches. Sue was suddenly aware of the fact that there were people very close to her back. She changed her stride, and Claire kept up with her. She told Claire in a low voice that upon her command they were to turn and walk swiftly backwards past anyone who was behind them. Claire by this time had realised that they were in danger. As directed, she turned on the spot when Sue gave the word, and they charged in between three men, who looked suitably surprised. They walked into a shop and remained there until they saw the three men walk away.

Nothing had happened. Or had it? Yes, it had. They had both sensed danger. The action that they took averted anything further from happening. However, what happened did happen. Sue felt a little foolish. Maybe the men were quite innocent. But perhaps they were not. The incident stayed with her and even to this day she does not like anyone getting close to her back as she walks. The scent of danger is activated all too quickly.

Memories do remain. People who have been mugged continue to live with the incident long after it is over. It is a frightening experience. It may happen to many people and so, like house burglary, is sadly part of routine enquiries for the police. However, for the victim, it is a unique event in their life and they need to deal with it to take away the trauma.

If you have been involved in a robbery and find that you carry memories that are painful or feel that you are living with a level of fear, do consider talking to someone about the situation. Don't stay a victim.

Domestic Abuse and other Abuse Settings

The isolation of domestic violence makes it no less real, and it is a crime. Such a crime occurring within the walls of the place you call home only adds to the total sense of violation and isolation. It is a crime that is not easy to prove.

People who assault those who are known to them are abusers. As such, they try to exercise power and control over others by making them feel scared and intimidated. This abuse may start with threats and then move into violent acts, which may become worse and more frequent over time. Please know that this sort of abuse is never your fault. Nobody has the right to abuse you in this way. All too often the victim is made to feel responsible and guilty for the abuse, but the problem lies with the abuser.

Those who suffer such abuse are often locked into the situation; there seems no escape. There is a fear that if they leave, the abuser will follow them, and the abuse will get worse. They may rely upon the abuser for financial support or worry about the fate of any children involved. It is all too common to hope that it will get better and to put off any action to leave or to speak up.

In 2002 a report to the Churches Together in Britain

and Ireland was published in a book called 'Time for Action.' I quote; "This book is not intended for easy reading in the comfort of a fireside chair! It is a book with a purpose and that purpose is to challenge, to call for action and justice. Its subject is sexual abuse and the Churches."

One of the questions it asks is as follows: "Who are those who survive sexual abuse?" It replies that the experience of sexual abuse in one form or another is far more common than acknowledged. Within our communities, within our churches, within our places of work may be found the survivors who remain mainly unrecognized. If such abuse is revealed, the following response is not unusual: -"I would never have guessed."

The following extract will help to set the scene.

""Most sexual abuse is not committed by extreme deviants; it often takes place within the home, from 'caring' people within the family and within other contexts in which there is an expectation of trust and care. In other words both those who are abused and those who abuse may be more ordinary than some would expect. Even genuine care and affection can develop a deviant or unhealthy nature, which it is why it is important that appropriate boundaries of behaviour are set and maintained."

The book continues:- "When abuse is in the family context it is often felt by victims and other family members that the 'secret' is best kept, because disclosure could lead to the 'blowing apart' of the family." It continues:- "It is these pressures which often prevent the victim from sharing – fearing they will destroy their family and faith network and believing it is better to suffer in secret. "(Time For Action. Published by Churches Together in Britain and Ireland.)

Many others have written about abuse including Penny Parks, author of The Counsellor's Guide to Parks Inner Child Therapy and Rescuing The 'Inner Child.' (Published by Souvenir Press in the Human Horizons Series), Park offers a framework from which broken lives that arise from abuse may be addressed. The books sets out the effects of trauma in the following extract. "When children experience trauma at the hands of trusted adults (especially family members) their emotional link with the adult world is severed, creating an emotional 'stop on time'. They are then left with three companions: guilt, fear and feelings of inadequacy. These three companions can stay on throughout their adult life governing part or all of their decision making." (P. Parks, Rescuing the 'Inner Child.)

This book can only briefly touch the edges of the depth of abuse; sexual, physical, emotional, spiritual and psychological. In the next case study we catch a glimpse of what is clearly a very great area of pain and distress.

CASE STUDY: Elaine and Peter and Family

Elaine lived with her husband and two children. Living in a large city with a circle of good friends they seemed much like any other family. Elaine noticed that Peter, her husband seemed stressed. She talked to him but he seemed reluctant to open up to her. She left the subject and they continued with their lives.

Some months later, she noticed further signs of stress in Peter. He started to be short-tempered with her and also the children, but again she thought that it would settle. Elaine devised all sorts of strategies to keep the peace during the week. Come the weekends, the tension really did begin to mount. The children noticed and remarked that daddy always seemed to be cross.

Eventually Elaine talked to Peter and challenged his behaviour with her and the children. He denied his behaviour and was angry with her for suggesting that he was less than a perfect father. Elaine let it drop until the situation at home became really unacceptable with frequent outbursts of anger from Peter. She then suggested that perhaps they both needed to go for some help.

Peter was very angry at the suggestion of outside help. It was a turning point in their relationship. It was the start of a domestic abuse situation. In addition to anger and harsh words during the day, their sexual relationship deteriorated rapidly into 'unacceptable' sex for Elaine.

This situation continued for some time. Why did Elaine allow this situation? Did she have a choice? The answer would be complex but at the top of the list was fear. Her security was within the marriage.

She relied upon Peter as a husband and father. The thought of moving on a step and challenging the marriage seemed too frightening for her.

Domestic abuse does not necessarily lead on to child abuse but the two may go, most painfully, hand in hand. Where domestic abuse takes place, the children almost inevitably become a part of the situation. They may only become the onlookers or the ones who hear but, in so doing, they become part of the abuse.

CASE STUDY continued: Elaine and Peter and Their Children

Consider again this family. Elaine was trying to block out the fact that Peter was continuing to be angry and indeed at times violent towards her and that their sexual relationship was no longer mutually acceptable.

Peter was harbouring dark thoughts that were alarming to him. But he did not know how to deal with the turmoil within him. If he could have talked through the dark thoughts that he held onto it would have allowed the light to come into the darkness of the thinking. Keeping it within his mind and mulling it over again and again made the thought pattern more intense.

Peter began to change. He has a certain look, noticed by those who know him. His emotions would build to a point and then explode in actions. Wrong actions. Unspoken actions. It would take another book to explain Peter's thinking, but as his emotions exploded he was destroying the people that he loved the most. They felt abused by his actions. The fabric of their safe family began to crumble. There then developed a silence. A deep family silence. The silence that speaks of pain, fear, anguish, and bewilderment.

Elaine wrote the following poem that describes her situation as the tension built up within the home.

THE SILENT PAIN

Do you know me? Damaged – dirty – torn.
Who will ever see, the pain,
The marks, the signs of touch, that were not love.
The sorrow and the tears,
The shame,
And then, the front, presented to the world.
The front, that speaks that all is well.
Inside – the pain.
They must not know.
Know that, behind the garments – clean and fresh
washed, sometimes twice
skin – cleansed and cleansed again.
Inside these outer vestments, lives a weary soul.
Accepting, but used and numb,
Afraid to speak.
Silent.
The pain within. No one must know.
One lives, one smiles, forgetting
jolted only, by the flashbacks.
Vivid. Plunged into that place
Where love becomes abuse.
 Held in so secret. God – please touch that part of me.

He will. I know he will.
Then, put on the garments, fresh and pure
and think no more.
For it is done.
Until it starts again.

While Elaine was coping with the abusive relationship with Peter, the children suffered. Domestic abuse creeps out and hurts the innocent. It creates a ripple effect within the family.

We hear of abuse cases via the media. You may observe that when such cases come to light, the one who has abused often finds it very difficult to own the crime. Those who work with abusers find that some simply cannot match up their actions with the report of what took place. That is part of the sickness of abuse. There is a distancing that goes on within the mind of the abuser. The problem for them is that if they acknowledged their part within the abuse, it might break their spirit forever. They cannot afford to let go and accept their part. They remain in denial.

The safeguarding of the young is a challenge for our society. The very nature of the offence seems to weave a tight web of secrecy.

The Every Child Matters: Change for Children Programme - is a government policy and aims to put in place a national framework to support the joining up of services, so that every child can achieve the five *Every Child Matters* outcomes which are stated below.

The Government's aim is for every child, whatever

their background or their circumstances, to have the support they need for them to be healthy, stay safe, enjoy and achieve, make a positive contribution, and achieve economic well-being.

This means that the organisations involved with providing services to children need to share information and work together to protect children and young people from harm and to help them achieve what they want in life.

In high-profile media situations, we hear of the very worst cases that slip through the net. What we don't hear about are the many situations when children are helped. The work of safeguarding children moves forward in active ways including preventative work with the parents.

However, the high ideals for the safeguarding of children still do not protect all children and abuse does take place. Take the father who whispers the words, "This is our little secret," followed by, "Don't tell your mum." Those words become part of the terrible secret world of the child who suffers abuse. If we have concerns, do we pass by on the other side for fear of involvement? What is our attitude? Are not our children, all children, of the greatest importance?

There are still some who feel that all this talk of abuse is overrated and overstated. Why are we making such a fuss about it now? This sort of thing has happened to past generations, and they all survived. Did they? At what cost? Child abuse leaves damaged individuals. Ask any therapist. I certainly see people still living with the memories of abusive situations. The memories may lay dormant for years and then some situation will 'trigger' them off.

Let us list the types of child abuse. There is child neglect, which is persistent or severe neglect of a child; the failure to protect a child from exposure to any kind of danger, including cold and starvation; extreme failure to carry out important aspects of care. Such neglect can result in the significant impairment of the child's health or development.

Then there is physical abuse. By this we mean actual or likely physical injury to a child, or failure to prevent physical injury (or suffering) to a child. This area also covers deliberate poisoning, suffocation, and Münchausen syndrome by proxy (Meadow, 1977), Factitious illness by proxy (Bools, 1996; Jones & Bools, 1999), or illness induction syndrome (Gray et al, 1995). These types of abuse are when a parent or carer deliberately makes the child ill and in need of medical attention, and can lead to the death of the child.

The causes of Munchausen by Proxy Syndrome vary greatly depending on the history and motives of the sufferer. In many cases, caregivers were abused or ignored and so suffered as children. The need for sympathy and attention becomes so all-encompassing that it surpasses basic parental instincts.

Because of the involvement of both the caregiver and the child, treatment for Munchausen by Proxy Syndrome is two-pronged. The first course of action is to remove the child from the harmful environment; once in a safe setting he or she can then be helped. Treatment may then be offered to the one who has abused; this is most effective when the perpetrator is able to admit his or her wrongdoing and actively seek recovery.

Child sexual abuse means actual or likely sexual exploitation of a child or adolescent. What do we mean by sexual abuse? Sexual abuse may not involve penetration. Fondling is still equally damaging: the emotional damage to the child is the same, and a pattern of fear and distrust is set in place. To further the definition, sexual abuse is when an adult involves a child in any activity from which the adult hopes, indeed expects, to derive sexual arousal. This does not mean that the child will have their body touched at all. They may witness the adult expose himself. They may witness a man with a hard erection beneath his trousers. It is often about the inappropriateness of the actions. For instance, a father or mother or some other person, often a family member may talk and look and touch their child in a consistently incorrect manner week after week. This process may all be part of grooming, which is when the abuser forms a relationship with the child, is seen by the child as a safe person, and then eventually turns on the child in an abusive way.

Emotional abuse damages the child or young person to different degrees. It can leave the child with severe adverse effects on their emotional and behavioural development. As they grow, they will carry fears with them, and there will be need to build up defence walls around themselves. Very often there is a sexual strand in this type of abuse. The damage often comes through in adult relationships.

Young people talk about car journeys when they felt trapped by the abuser. A certain tone of the voice may be used which is frightening to the child. Children may become part of the adult world in such settings. They innocently become part of a secret world. All this is abusive and may stay with the child into adulthood. If this is the case and damage was done, when the child reaches adulthood, sexual relationships may be difficult to form. A child exposed to such situations will carry the scar, and their own sexual relationships will need to be helped and healed.

CASE STUDY continued: Elaine, Peter and Their Children

In the case of Elaine and her marriage to Peter, as she retreated into her own world of fear due to their abusive relationship, so Peter, feeling misunderstood and pushed away started little rituals with his one daughter. He did not openly abuse her in the way that some understand the word abuse. He had little chats with her. He would walk up to her from behind and touch her arm. There was a certain smile. His manner and the context of these encounters made this child feel most uncomfortable. This all took place in the 'safety' of their home.

Elaine then noticed a change in her husband's

behaviour. The outbursts of anger became less frequent and he became withdrawn and cold. Control was a big issue for Peter. To avoid loss of control, he simply went deep within himself.

But what was happening to his feelings? He kept them well hidden until he could no longer contain them. His one release was through sex. Sex for him was an expression of those feelings. His body language was sexual, and he shook with emotion in order to contain what was building up inside him. He was like a pressure cooker with the weight firmly in place.

Here was a man who would never see himself as an abuser. Indeed, others would not have seen him as an abuser. He is not alone. There are other men who follow the same pattern of behaviour, of course with variations.

Peter could not accept any wrongness in his actions. He simply could not. If he did so, the very core of him would be shattered. It would be too dangerous by far to accept responsibility for his actions.

One must always remember that the children are the innocents in all cases. As adults, we are responsible for our behaviour. In such a distressing situation, there will be a scar stamped on each family member.

As if it is not bad enough for the immediate family, this sort of abusive situation can leak out into the extended family. In the case of such abuse, while the immediate 'victims' are still having to cope with past abuse and are working to find a way through their own pain, they may have to watch this dreadful process happening all over again within the extended family.

If the core family reveal to anyone what has been happening, the chances are very high that they will not be believed. Added to this, their desire to be made well is the priority. Being made well involves seeking professional help and then putting it all behind them. As the individual begins to leave behind the awfulness of the abusive situation, they will be very reluctant to draw attention to the possible danger that might face younger friends or indeed family members. This is why abuse within the family is so often never challenged.

For any who have been abused in such a way, some words of encouragement: face the abuse, seek professional help, and begin to own and acknowledge what has taken place. It will not be easy, and at times you may want to put all the memories away as you work through your pain. It may be a case of working through this in stages. You can come through to the other side. Hold on in there and be determined not to remain a victim.

We have used the example of a man as the one who abuses but of course women abuse too. In these situations the need to bring this behaviour to light is just as pressing as are the reasons for keeping it well hidden.

People who have suffered abuse express the view that they have missed out on life. They have been so taken up with survival and developing their own way of living that life seems to have passed them by. This can make them very angry as well as sad.

Some feel a need to do something to address the loss. Their experience may lead them into areas where they are able to listen and help others who have experienced abuse. They may write or talk about areas of abuse. Their desire is to help others to recover and so feel that their experience was not totally negative.

For some the following words may be of some comfort. With acknowledgement of past abuse and as the individual begins painfully to find healing, it really can seem that one is released from darkness and that one is no longer a prisoner. Years on, unexpected blessings may pour upon the person. They feel that the years of pain are being repaid with unexpected love and joy. It is very beautiful when this takes place.

"He has sent me to bind up the broken hearted, to proclaim freedom for the captives and release from darkness for the prisoners" Isaiah 61:1.

"I will repay you for the years the locusts have eaten" Joel 2:25.

To those who have abused: acknowledge it; make amends; be contrite. Not to do so, will almost certainly mean that as the family grows up they will draw away from you. They will carry pain but, with help, joy will come back into their lives. It may never do so for the one who has abused.

Rape and Sexual Assault

For all that one thinks of this as a crime that is aimed at females, there are of course males who are badly hurt by such violent actions. They too need to be heard and cared for in the same sort of way.

Being raped or sexually assaulted is a very distressing experience and the effects can last for many years. Each person who is attacked like this will respond differently but there will be some common factors in every case.

The victim will experience very intense emotions following such an attack. They usually find it difficult to sleep, eating is either too little or too much, concentration is usually poor, and there is a tendency to withdraw from other people.

Many will show the rape trauma syndrome. This begins with acute stress immediately following the rape. There will also be some or all of the following: fear, anger, shock, self-blame, disbelief.

It is good if the person can cry and say what happened very shortly after the rape. However, some may hide their reactions. If they continue to hide the feelings, the shock continues to go inward, and the person begins to freeze emotionally. It is as if they begin to die inside. Should this happen, it is very difficult indeed to reach them. They will become silent and will freeze in both body and mind.

This reaction to rape is known as the silent rape reaction. The silent rape reaction is sometimes seen in women who were abused as children. When children, they simply did not speak about it through fear and, as adults, the same is true. They so fear the reaction of those around them that they seal it all in. They have even more reason to seal in the emotions and remain silent.

After a rape, the victim may begin to have nightmares, irrational fears, or restless activity. They will often feel dirty. Hence much washing and changing of sheets and clothes takes place. They may feel that the whole world can see through them. There may well be a reluctance to go out into the world and mix with others.

It is important to report incidences of rape. By telling someone else, the dreadfulness of the situation will come into the light. You will then be helped step by step. At this stage, the shock of such a crime makes many feel numb and unable to make decisions. Thus they need to be led on in the process. There will be the risk of sexually transmitted diseases and pregnancy. Anyone who has been raped or sexually attacked needs to be treated with great care. They need to feel safe and thus to be with safe people.

CASE STUDY: Pat

Pat was an innocent child who viewed the world with cheerfulness. Living on a farm, she loved to walk in the countryside delighting in the sights and sounds around her. She talked freely with people who came to the farm, and life was good for her. One day, her world changed.

She was fifteen years old. Her cousins were visiting the farm. The adults were in the house, and the children and young people were sitting around on the lawn. Her cousin, a young man of seventeen, suggested that she go with him into the barn. Off she went with him. What happened inside the barn was to have a bearing upon Pat for the rest of her life. Her cousin raped her. He said it was for a bit of a lark. She was a trusting soul and went with the lark.

The cousins visited the farm every so often, and each time there was a visit to the barn. Her cousin spoke words like "our secret" and "you know you enjoy it" to Pat. Pat knew that she did not enjoy it, but she was too afraid to say anything to anyone. Pat became a frightened girl. She no longer walked in the country. There was fear in every strange place for Pat.

One day, to her horror, she realized that she was pregnant. She managed to tell her mother, who went into overdrive. Doctors were seen. They spoke to Pat but she refused to speak to them. She had gone into silent rape reaction.

Pat ended up having an abortion. Four years later, she had a breakdown. Again, the doctors tried to get her to talk. The rape, followed by the abortion, had sealed the pain deep within her.

Some twelve years later, Pat decided to go for help. Her life was being ruled by fear. She was unable to have any sort of relationship with a man. If he so much as touched her, she would freeze. Bit by bit, over the years Pat began to remember the trauma. She had effectively sealed it all up. Slowly, but painfully slowly and in her own time, she began to remember and talk.

Her recovery was on the way, but the healing was a very long, ongoing process.

Murder and Manslaughter

Losing someone through such a violent act is devastating. There will be many ingredients that make the sum of the whole in such a situation. The circumstances will vary, but the pain is acute in all.

We have all watched tragic situations unfold through the media when there is a murder or a death through manslaughter. The pain in the eyes of those who are close to the victim speaks volumes. Losing someone through a violent act is a devastating experience. Everyone experiences the bereavement differently, and often feelings change from day to day. Within the UK, there are good services available to come alongside anyone in such a ghastly situation. Those left grieving need all the support that others can offer to them at such a time.

If a person, especially a child, is missing and there is a time gap while a search takes place, the waiting is intolerable for the loved ones of the missing person. Again, they need all the help they can get from family and the professionals around them. The dreaded news then comes: a body has been found. Following on from this, someone will have to identify the body. No easy task. I have known fathers who shoulder this task to help to shield a tiny bit of pain from their wives. In due course there will be the return of the personal belongings of the victim. The police often can do an excellent job in the following pain-filled days. There is so much to do, and yet disbelief and numbness prevail. In due course, there will be a funeral to arrange. It is a time of waiting and turmoil. It is like being in one's worst imaginable nightmare. How can life go on ever again?

A different situation arises when the missing person is not found. The families are left with no closure. Tragic though it may be, a funeral provides an ending and is a signal to move into the next stage of grief. If no body is found, there is no funeral. The grief remains stuck within the hearts of those who loved that missing person. It is endlessly painful and tragic.

Added to the grief are the other feelings of the people who are left behind. They often feel isolated and helpless. The world may start to seem hostile and uncaring. Feelings of guilt may surface. "Why am I still here?" is the sort of question they ask. They have survived, but the one they love has not. "If only" is another saying. "If only I had driven her." "If only I had got there sooner." "If only I had told him how much I love him." The suddenness of the death is cruel.

Looking for a motive and perpetrator will be the job of the police. There will be many hours of questions for the devastated family. Who did it? Why did they do it? As we know from the media, not all crimes are solved. The gap of time between the funeral and a court case will vary. Listening to the details of a trial is harrowing for the family. Having to see the accused in the dock is a part of the process of grieving. Depending on the outcome of the trial, one sees differing reactions from family and friends.

The torment surrounding these situations is endless and can affect one's health, faith, values, friendships, and family life. Some may suffer from the loss of the ability to function at work, at home, or in school. Suddenly, one notices every crime reported on the media. Interviews on crime-related topics may inflame one's sense of injustice. The grief just goes on and on. There are so many questions. What does one do with the possessions of the deceased? What does one do with their bedroom?

Sibling Grief

This is a very delicate area. When a brother or sister dies, family members may process the sudden reality of the death in different ways and at different stages and times. Initially, the focus is often on the parents. Somehow, siblings are left out. The parents who would once comfort them are right out of comfort. They are grief-filled and may well not have the capacity to be the comforters.

Comments from Siblings

The following are words and feelings expressed by siblings in this situation. High on the emotional list is anger. One brother stated: "Verbally I would lash out at everyone. I couldn't express any other feeling. My sister was gone and it was the world's fault."

Often experienced is guilt leading to such questions

as: "Why am I still here? Why wasn't it me? What did I do wrong for this to happen to my brother?"

A sense of fear may prevail: "When my brother was murdered, I thought, who is next in our family? All of a sudden our family was a target, and we can't hide and protect ourselves from further harm."

Sadly, there may be a rapid loss of innocence: "I'm no longer a child, it seems. Murder made me grow up too fast, and I lost a big part of my childhood that I can never get back."

Siblings may become protective of their parents: "When my sister was murdered, I had to be strong for my parents. They needed me. It took a while for me to think of my own grief."

And then loneliness: "I had lost my best friend – my brother. Life will never be the same again. I don't know if I want to go on living." Depression may creep up: "I don't want to get up. I don't want to see anyone. No one knows what to say to me. I don't want to look anyone in the eye. I can't trust anyone."

How Parents and Other Family Might Help the Siblings Left Behind

Accept your child's feelings. Allow them the space to grieve in their own way and encourage them to express feelings. Share your grief with your child – but don't give the impression that you hurt more than they do. Grieve together. Spend quality time with the children who are left.

Each child needs individual acceptance. Help them to nurture their own identity. Find healthy ways to remember your loved one. Perhaps find special photos and make an album. Encourage the children who are left to write, paint, and talk.

Please don't take down family pictures. You still have a family, and your lost child is still part of that family. To take them away may be interpreted by a sibling as a total loss of family. Please get help as needed. You can't do this all on your own.

How does one go on living after such a tragedy? Those who are left with such grief have to find their own way forward. The time and the method they choose will be right for each of them.

Over the years, the media has shown us how some people offer their forgiveness to the perpetrators. If you have lost someone very dear to you through a criminal act, you will, as a family, have experienced a sense of great vulnerability along with a host of emotions. Some talk about the need to forgive. Others find this concept quite impossible. Talking to others who have lost loved family members in such tragic circumstances can be helpful, at the right time for each person. The aim is not to become a victim. Listening to others and how they have coped may help you to see that one day you may find a tiny shaft of light.

Helpful follow up

SAMM (Support After Murder and Manslaughter) ~ Cranmer House, 39 Brixton Road, London SW9 6DZ. Tel. 020 7735 3838 www.samm.org.uk

Compassionate Friends ~ 53 North Street, Bristol BS3 1EN. Tel. 0117 914 4368 www.tcf.org.uk

Bristol Crisis Service for Women, PO Box 654, Bristol BS991XH Tel. 0117 9251119

This number is the national helpline for women.

ChildLine, Freepost 1111, London N10BR   Tel. 0800 1111

NAPAC (the National Association for People Abused in Childhood), c/o BSS, Union House, Shepherd's Bush Green, London W12 8UA

CSSA (Christian Survivors of Sexual Abuse), BM-CSSA, London WC1N 3XX

Chapter Four

Premature Death

Premature death is deeply distressing for all concerned; the grief is raw and the pain acute. We consider here reasons for premature death in the young, but of course premature death in an adult is also filled with pain.

Miscarriage

Each year in the UK, hundreds of thousands of women are affected by miscarriage. In the vast majority of cases, there is no way to prevent miscarriage. Having a miscarriage does not mean that you won't be able to get pregnant again, and most women go on to have a successful pregnancy later.

The medical definition of miscarriage is 'the spontaneous loss of a pregnancy before twenty four weeks'. In the event of a miscarriage, support and information from the medical profession, as well as from family and friends as appropriate, will be needed. For the woman, it may be the first time that she has ever been to hospital and the sights, sounds, and smells may be distressing, let alone the pain and discomfort that she feels. And do not forget the partner who watches, wanting to help but powerless. It is a traumatic time for them both. There may be a great desire to 'do something'. Partners who watch have spoken about the feeling of being 'helpless'. They are onlookers and feel they have handed over all control to strangers.

With miscarriage, there will be grief as intense as after any other bereavement. Many women describe a feeling of numbness and emptiness. Some couples withdraw, feeling alone and isolated; others may wish to talk about it. There is one universal message to those who comfort a woman who has recently miscarried. Please do not say, "Never mind, you will have another one." That is not helpful. Why?

The miscarried baby needs to be mourned. That child is a child in his or her own right. They are special and precious and cannot be 'replaced'. Yes, the mother may have another child in due course, but at that moment the loss, rightly so, will be focused upon the lost child. That baby was a little person to that mother and father. The little one had become part of the thoughts and dreams of those parents. That baby is then no more.

It is so important to have time to mourn in whatever way is right for parents. Their mourning can take many forms. You should receive help over how you act in the days immediately following a miscarriage, depending upon where it took place and how many weeks you were into your pregnancy. You may want to name the baby and have some sort of service in remembrance of the child. It is a personal matter, and you need time and help to work out what is right for you. Some hospitals have a book of remembrance in their chapel so that the name of the baby may be written down and so be remembered year by year in prayer.

For all too many women who have had a miscarriage, nothing of any significance was done in remembrance of their child. Years later, they realise that they are still grieving for the lost baby. The following case history will illustrate this dilemma.

CASE STUDY: Joan

Joan came to a 'Baby Loss' service in a church near to her home. This service was held every year so that parents who had lost children could come and remember them. During the service there was an opportunity to write the name of the lost child on a piece of paper and, at a certain point in the service, the names of all the children were spoken out and committed to the loving care of God. A candle could be lit and placed with other candles at the front of the church.

Joan had miscarried forty years previously. Forty years on, it still worried her that the baby had never been properly laid to rest. She came to the service after having talked to one of the leaders of the service, so she was prepared and knew what she wanted to do. Not knowing the sex of her baby, she named the baby

91

'Max' and wrote that name upon the piece of paper. She sat through the service with tears streaming down her face. Listening to the name of her child being read out was a profound experience for her. She then made the long walk (long to her) to light her candle and placed it lovingly with the other little flames of light.

Speaking to me afterwards, she talked about a great sense of lightness coming upon her. It felt as if a weight had been lifted from her and a light had come into a dark place within her. It had been a significant experience for her.

The Death of a Child

The death of a baby or young child is also deeply distressing for all concerned. Stillbirth, cot death, or the deaths of young children are experiences filled with distress and grief. Perhaps the most often asked question in these circumstances is why.

In the case of stillbirth, listen to a mother who has given birth to a perfectly formed baby and held that baby in her arms. Note, the baby is perfectly formed, but without life. The pain is raw, the sense of disbelief tangible.

Cot death (otherwise known as Sudden Infant Death Syndrome – SIDS) is a shocking happening. The acute awfulness of finding your precious child not breathing in their cot is followed by a host of emotions. Those who talk about such an event see it as a terrible nightmare experience. The mother and father are left in utter confusion and disbelief. They need much help and care in the initial weeks and then much understanding and compassion as the weeks go by. It is every parent's dread. The question, "why?" is asked again and again.

Some babies die in early infancy. The family has started to get to know that child and then, like a puff of smoke, the light is extinguished. In the case of sudden death, there is no opportunity for preparation or anticipatory grieving. In the case of a child who is ill or has some major life-threatening problem, the family will live with the knowledge that this life will not continue forever. They start to experience bereavement before the child dies. Nonetheless, the agony is still just as fierce when the child does die. No preparation can take away the wrench and the feeling of loss.

The care of such children is all-encompassing for the parents. They want to give their all to that child. Life may be full of conflict. If they have other children, they will feel wrenched from them. Parents in such situations talk about the guilt of not being with their other children. They experience stress and anxiety. In some circumstances, hospice care is all-important in the life of such families. Hospice care takes the whole family into account, and this is what needs to be considered at every stage by those who surround a family at this time.

A child who is dying may well have questions about what is happening. They need to be able to express their hopes and their fears. The adults need support as they answer such questions with honesty, simplicity, and reassurance. Remember, hearing is usually one of the last faculties to be lost, so words of love and comfort may be continued to the end.

Sisters and brothers of a dying child should not be excluded. Experience shows that it is important for them to be involved. They too have questions and views. To be excluded may lead to deep-seated distress and anger for them in years to come.

We may try to protect children from pain, but to exclude them from the death of a brother or sister can play havoc with their minds. They may create some sort of fantasy, and such fantasies can be more terrible than reality. Reality can be more contained and controlled in the memory. Fantasy easily runs out of control.

The role of the extended family in such situations is a delicate one. The grandparents are in a very painful position. They are watching their grandchild die as well as watching their own child going through such agony. Of course, it is up to the parents to decide to what extent the wider family are to be involved. The parents may need the help of the professionals in such decisions. Whatever is decided, someone needs to care and listen to the grandparents and other family members as needed. If they are given support, they in turn will be better able to help pick up the pieces in years to come. These situations can make or break families.

A most helpful book in this area is *Just My Reflection: Helping parents to do things their way when a child dies* by Sister Frances Dominica, and published by Darton, Longman and Todd.

Facing Sudden Death in an Older Teenager

CASE STUDY: Tom

Tom was the youngest of four children. When he was twelve years old, his brother Mark, aged fourteen, died from a heart attack. He just fell down when they were out playing with a ball and never recovered.

The rest of the family were in severe shock. The two older siblings, both girls, came home and helped their parents with all that needed to be done. They then returned to where they lived to continue their lives. Tom was left at home with his parents to continue his life. But life had changed. How could he go on living? His parents seemed different. They were different. The house was still and silent. Tom wanted to go into Mark's bedroom but could not bring himself to do so.

Years later, Tom went to see his doctor who suggested that he see a therapist. Tom suffered from depression. The depression had started when he was in his early teens. As he told his story to the counsellor, he said again and again, "I could not add my pain to that of my parents. It was not safe to do so." Tom had grieved alone. But it was not a helpful grief process for him. He had lost his identity. He had experienced a range of emotions including anger, grief, guilt, and abandonment. In order to deal with these feelings, he suppressed them. This denial led him into depression. No one recognised his loss. He was coping with the loss of his brother as well as the loss of functional parents. He then took on the guilt of being the one son who was still alive. He felt he could never be as good as his brother and consequently felt he let his parents down.

Tom began to work through his feelings and reactions. He had tried to be his brother but had failed. As he discovered himself, he realised he had something to offer to the world, and he began to live with himself again. He need not have gone through all that aloneness if someone had seen what was happening to the whole family. We need to pay attention to every family member who is left behind after premature death. They each need time and space to grieve. They need to talk.

Children and young people do tragically die in various ways. How the families cope depends upon their own resources as well as on the help of those around them. In the initial days, as the families live in grief, they need individuals to be with them. It takes great care and sensitivity as one listens and walks in that grief with them. Words are often not needed. It is the company of another that can be of such help. Be prepared to take the anger and pain of individuals should you be in that role. They need to express what they feel and when they feel it. The first year is very important for anyone in such a situation. It will shape the years to come.

Useful contacts.

Child Death Helpline ~ Great Ormond Street for Children Hospital. Tel. 0800 282986 www.childdeathhelpline. org.uk

SANDS (Stillbirth And Neonatal Death Society) ~ 28 Portland Place, London Q1B 1LY. Tel. 020 7436 5881 www.uk-sands.org

Cot Death Society ~ 4 West Mills Yard, Kennet Road, Newbury RG14 5LP.
Tel. 0845 601 0234 www.cotdeathsociety.org.uk

Sudden Infant Death Syndrome – SIDS ~ Artillery House, 11–19 Artillery Row,
London SW1P 1RT Tel. 020 7222 8001

Ashley Jolly Sudden Death Trust, SADS UK ~ 22 Rowhedge, Brentwood, Essex CM13 2TS
Tel. 01277 230642 www.sadsuk.org

Chapter Five

Separation and Divorce

Picture two pieces of paper stuck together. In your mind now tear one piece of paper from the other. You will be left with shreds of paper. Some have described divorce like these shreds of paper. For others, it seems that the process is very much less painful.

You may be reading this while experiencing the process of divorce. How would you describe it? Some describe it as a bad dream that gradually and painfully begins to shape into reality. From the bad dream to the reality, a great host of feelings and emotions are experienced. For some people, it is the first time that they have felt the strength of their emotions.

CASE STUDY: Sue and Andrew

Sue came to me first. She had been to see her GP who had suggested counselling. During the first session, she described an all-too-usual marriage pattern. Andrew, her husband and the father of their two children, appeared tired and distracted at home. He was working long hours and complained that he did not want to be got at upon his return from work. Sue, on the other hand, was eager to see him at the end of the day. Her life was full of little children and all the business of motherhood. She would have been so pleased to have some help at the end of her child-filled days as well as being able to converse with him. This pattern had continued for some twelve years, and Sue felt it was getting worse. In the second week, she told me that Andrew would like to see me.

The session with Andrew was sadly revealing. He had found another woman and was seeing her on a regular basis. Yes, he was distracted when at home. He did not know what to do. We talked and he was able to unburden a whole host of feelings. He was in great conflict. The thought of walking out on Sue was a recurring one. He did not know if he could do such a thing to Sue and his children, yet he really could no longer cope with his relationship with Sue. Her world revolved around the children. He felt pushed out and excluded. There was little physical, let alone sexual, touch left within the relationship. As the years went by, he'd felt more and more alone and in need of attention. It is such a familiar pattern and, unless faced and dealt with after the first warning signs, can often prove to be irreversible.

Sadly, this was so in this instance. One morning, Andrew left for work and did not return. He telephoned Sue on the first evening and told her he had to work late and would not be home that evening. Sue was alarmed with reason. His absence continued into night two and by then Sue just knew. She became frantic, and a series of telephone calls were made. The panic and tension were becoming acute. She contacted her parents, who lived some little distance away, and they came at once. It was decided that they would stay to help sort out the situation.

Sue started to text Andrew. He ignored the messages. All the while, he was getting more and more determined not to let the messages cut into him with pangs of guilt. He softened momentarily on day four and sent Sue a text saying that he would be home later that evening. When he arrived, he was met not only by his wife but also his parents–in–law. He was furious. He stormed around the house and ended up taking a suitcase full of his clothes with him as he left.

The saga continued. Anger, pain, disbelief, fear, anxiety, guilt, numb shock, sorrow, and tears. A sense of unreality. This was not happening. It was all a bad dream.

But it was not. It was all too late for them. Andrew's mind was elsewhere, and he could not face the reality of his relationship with Sue and the responsibility of fatherhood. He moved in with his new woman. An undemanding, uncomplicated existence.

So what then? Sue began a process where she wondered if he would return, became angry, determined he was not going return, all the while accompanied by words, words and more words from parents, parents-in-law, friends, and family. "Why don't you; perhaps if; if only; we never saw it coming; well dear we were concerned." Guilt poured upon guilt. Sue became indignant. "What about my needs?" Having children is a life-changing experience. It went on and on in her mind.

Then she slipped into denial, imagining he would walk back through the door. He would smile, say 'sorry, I don't know what came over me. Can we talk, work it out?' You may want to hug him, smile. But maybe you will be frozen. Frozen in hurt and pain and indignation. So very alone. There is even aloneness when with the children. Will you ever feel like you used to feel? How did you used to feel? That is the scary bit. You are no longer able to connect with the person you were before this nightmare.

Recurring nightmares, waking up with a jolt and to realise that the nightmare is reality. You call upon God. Where was He in all of this? Meanwhile, the world goes on as normal. How can it? Normal for you is lost. You have no normal.

Then there are the strange conversations with the man you had married. He looks the same, yet he seems a stranger. Once trusted, now traitor. No longer there to depend upon. He is gone. But he is not dead. There is no ending point. No funeral. No official goodbye point. No official grieving from others. So much to decide and yet to make decisions seems impossible. How can one decide upon something that one does not want?

Emotions that hurt so much. Intense, deep, all pervasive. The pain going right through you and then stabbing into your body. A pain deep within.

The loss is unbearable; so you walk in unreality for some of the time. That is a cushion; it eases the pain a tiny bit. No one is very interested. Once they have heard the news, they may feel sorry, say they are sorry, and then life rolls on for them. They perhaps offer to have the children while you sort things out. Ten years of marriage reduced to 'things that need to be sorted out'. Then you think, it is more than ten years. You knew him for much longer – knew him when he was at university. The carefree chap who stole your heart. You stop thinking. It hurts too much.

Endless days roll into endless weeks and onto endless months. Will you survive? You have survived life thus far. Will this break you?

If you have experienced such a situation, how did you cope? How has it changed you? Trust is usually a big issue. Depending upon your circumstances, you may or may not be able to look back yet. Wherever you are on your journey you will be changed in some way. Picture again the two pieces of paper stuck together and then torn apart; two clean sheets of paper do not emerge. It is rather like this for a couple who tear apart. What is your end result? Do you have a void that is filled with unwanted feelings?

Your story may sound a little like the following: a single mum, two children, husband with another woman; access sorted, working full time now, maintenance payments a real burden for the ex; new friends emerging as most of your old ones have left you to find your way as a single parent. You can't look too far ahead; live for each day. But you need to start to find you. Who do you see in the mirror each day?

Look in the mirror. Look into your eyes. Look at the pain. Watch the tears pour down from such sad eyes. Accept the terrible sadness. Hold yourself in the sadness. This is you. A very sad you. The void contains sadness. What can you do with sadness? Hold it for now. Look again. You see pain, hurt for you and your children. You still see disbelief that this has happened. Face that and say to yourself that this is reality. Face all the other feelings. Really look into yourself and face them.

Then bit by bit decide what you are going to do about them. Are you going to live with that pain-filled void or are you going to move on in your grief? You are in grief. You may not have identified that your void was grief-filled. Pain, anger, disbelief, shock, numbness, and pleading. All these and more – all related to grief. So is it time to move on? There is no corporate grieving. There is no funeral, and no spot to mark the end. Nowhere to lay flowers.

But you do have your two children. How are they doing? Can you begin to make new memories with them? As you do so, can you acknowledge the loss of their family unit with them? Face the hurt with them. They may not be very old, but you can demonstrate the loss in positive ways. A visit to the sea; draw faces in the sand; express the fact that you are sorry daddy is not here but we can all still have fun. As you talk, you will make the positives. A picnic – no daddy to carry the backpack – so you all do your bit, backpacks for all. You are, in a most symbolic way, sharing the load of grief and turning it into something positive. The three of you can share the load. You really can do it. First holiday – don't try to be too brave –this is when you look to family or very good friends. They help to fill the void. They make new memories with you and your children.

The days roll on. The day comes when that bit of paper falls upon your floor. You are divorced. Emotions and feelings flood your body. Need time to be on your own. Take it all in. But hopefully the void has started to be filled with new feelings. Yes, the shock is still there as you read the final bit of paper. Work with what is going on. Look into the mirror. This is the time to take time for you. It may only be an evening. Do something for yourself. Fill the void with a positive.

It is now also the time to think about letting go, forgiving. For some, they feel the need to forgive themselves as well as the ex-partner. At the right time and in the right place and manner, it is necessary to forgive. To hold onto the pain and anger will hurt you still further. Remember, forgiveness is not saying that what happened did not matter. It did matter very much and still does matter. But you have to allow the person to go and you forgive.

Chapter Six

Roots

Songs are written about the days of one's childhood. In the words of their songs, singers take us to the mountains of their childhood and recall the people and events of those happy sun filled days; the range of hills that served as their childhood playground; the companions with whom they played; and the family around them. There were log fires, soup upon the stove, and granny sitting in the rocking chair, waiting with arms open wide to hug boys with grazed knees. The traditions of the women-folk were passed on to the girls. They were taught to sew and knit and bake bread as well as to produce all the known and much-loved recipes.

"It seemed back then that anything I wanted could come true." Words like that conjure up a picture of being cocooned by a loving family who somehow make everything feel all right. The innocence of childhood, not to be disrupted, not to be taken away, not to ever be underestimated in the strong foundation that it provided to those who were fortunate enough to have experienced it.

The mountains may have been green fields, hard pavements, or dusty tracks. The point is, if we have the right ingredients as we grow up, that is very special and provides us with a backdrop for the rest of our lives, however smooth or turbulent they may be.

As we grow up, we mould into a certain culture. That culture teaches us customs. Quite simply, this involves how to live life with a certain group of people. This may be in China, the Middle East, Africa, North America, or in the hills of Scotland. Each and every place has its culture with its ways and its sayings. There is an order and a pattern for what to do and how to do it. We may not be aware of such rules for living as we grow up. They just happen around us, and we fall into the pattern of them.

What happens when a person is taken away from all that is familiar to them? If the transition is orderly and planned, it is easier to adapt to new ways. In a new situation, one learns to do things in different ways though still often staying within the known culture. The pull of the familiar is very strong indeed. The language, the religion, the sayings, and the ways of doing things, the humour, the smells, the sights, the sounds, the food, the customs, the dress code, and the look of the people — all add to the rich tapestry of culture.

If one is uprooted in urgent, undignified haste from one's culture, the consequences can be quite traumatic and long lasting. Think of all the refugees. Such people may fear persecution on the basis of their race, religion, nationality, or membership in a particular social or political group. They are forced from their countries by war, civil conflict, political strife, or gross human rights abuses. There were an estimated 14.9 million refugees in the world in 2001 – people who had crossed an international border to seek safety – and at least 22 million internally displaced persons who had been uprooted within their own countries.

Leaving aside the politics of any of this, how do they cope with their loss?

Throughout history, people have fled their homes to escape persecution. We see that when this happens, it is instinctive to group together until they find a safe place to settle; and so the culture continues, albeit in desperate circumstances such as a refugee camp. For others, if the place really is such that they can settle, the culture is built into daily life around them, and the whole look of the area will change. There is a strong pull to be with the known. Of course, the edges get blurred as different cultures rub shoulders together, but there will always be that basic instinct to go back to the places of one's childhood, to find the land of one's childhood with all that it may represent. If people cannot physically do that, then they will remember and talk about such places with far away looks in their eyes.

Our individual story is woven into a people, into a culture. If you have moved and changed countries, to meet up with those who have a similar story may be very helpful. As you talk and share with like-minded people, memories of past years come to you, jokes and tales are told; you become part of that culture. There is a common, indefinable oneness. Such encounters may help to fill a void in your life.

Let us consider several groups of people who have had to adapt to change. In past generations, children of British parents who lived abroad were sent 'home' to be educated. This meant a long journey by sea and, once in the UK, the children stayed for the duration with only occasional visits from parents. After the Second World War, air travel became a travel option, and by the sixties a small army of children were flying to and fro from distant lands in order to be educated in the UK. In those days, it was considered safe for these young people to fly around the world with little or no supervision. They became accustomed to air travel. That was not a problem; the potential for problems arose in their emotional ability to handle the different lifestyles between holidays and school as well as the emotional highs and lows of leaving home again and again and returning to their place of education.

CASE STUDY: Harriet

Harriet was sent to school at the age of ten. Her parents lived in East Africa where she had enjoyed a relaxed outdoor style of life attending a small English-speaking school. She had vivid memories of her first term at her new school in the UK; but on the whole, made the adjustment well and began to settle into this new way of life. Then came the Christmas holidays and with feelings of excitement she flew back to her parents. Back in her old life, she felt happy but there was the looming thought that it would all end soon. Sure enough it did, and she returned to the UK four weeks later. She repeated this process once or twice a year for the next seven years. (It was not possible to return home every holiday. Her mother arranged for her to stay with extended family or friends. Not a happy solution for her at the time or in the future as she was left with issues around being not wanted and being a bother.) However, she became a confident and able traveller taking waits and changes in travel arrangements in her stride, but what was happening to her emotions and feelings?

When the journey back to school was a day or so away, she described how she began the emotional countdown; this was to prepare her mind before having to part from her parents and her life in Africa. At the airport, farewells over, she immersed herself in a book as she waited to board the plane; she took her mind to another place. The next stage was as she stepped into the plane. Feelings were numbed at that point; there were no more feelings allowed. She remained in that state of numbness for the entire flight, and this continued for several days after she had arrived back at school. She was then able to switch back and was emotionally geared for school life again.

I have observed that children who had such experiences developed what I call the 'overseas boarding school look, talk and walk.' As they made the transition back into school life their attitude was one of indifference; nothing was going to rock their tightly held in emotions; no situation was going to weaken their resolve to be strong. They shrugged off any hurtful comments and acted in a cool manner.

For the most part, these children adapted to this lifestyle; there were certainly many positive outcomes for them. There was street credibility to be gained when they returned to school with a wonderful tan. They were the richer for the diverse experiences. These children became good at living in two very different cultures and, in order to make that transition, they could easily press the switch and block the emotions. For most, this ability has remained with them into adult life; useful at times but not helpful at others.

These children 'survived' but at what price? For some the lack of stability of a home base led to insecurity. Just where did they belong? School became their one place of stability. School did not move; as their parents moved from country to country. For the girls, marriage at an early age provided the stability that was so lacking. Saying 'goodbye' in adult years could be difficult as they found themselves going back onto automatic pilot before any significant departure. So for all that there were positives, both sexes have been left with a mountain of issues related to the emotional highs and lows of their childhood.

Take another group: the Armed Services. There is a culture unique to those who serve in them. The customs, the vocabulary and the order in which words are put, the uniforms, the instant recognition of certain actions at certain time, the sounds, and the whole rhythm of the life and ways of the armed services make it difficult for that transfer into civilian life at the end of a time of service. There is a certain comfort within 'The Mess'. Entertainment, be it for rank and file or at officer level, is all within known boundaries. Your mates look out for you. Your fellow officers do likewise. The basics are provided for you within well-oiled machinery. Leaving that well organized, known, and trusted culture may be a shock in spite of any preparation that is provided to soften the leap from one life to another.

What then for those who have lived life in a monastic way? The 'I leaped over the wall' bit still happens today. The world seems a very unsafe place for those in this situation. The adjustment to the new culture is very difficult. The loss of the pace and routine of life is very sharp. The world seems so noisy, so unpredictable, and so unsafe. Who can one trust? The peace and security that was found within the walls of the monastery or convent are no more. They are very alone in being able to share anything of their lost culture with others who have had a parallel experience for there are no clubs or streets full of ex-religious.

Be kind and listen to them should you meet them on your journey through life. If you are one of them, do talk about your past life. Find people that you trust and speak out your hurt, pain, and loss. There will be a level of the loss of identity. The wearing of a habit is an instant way into conversing with others. The habit spelt out who you were and what you stood for. Without it, who are you now?

Where and how do such people fit into our way of life? Clothes are a challenge. No more comfortable covering of the body. It feels very vulnerable to walk down the street in a short skirt and exposed arms. The food is very different for many, very rich and of such variety. What about the hair? This is especially true for the woman. The cost of everything, including a decent hair cut, is all part of the culture shock. Where to live? Having lived surrounded by others, it may feel very lonely when you leave. Yet the paradox is that you long to be alone. There are just too many people about and too much noise. There is also the matter of finances; how to fund this new way life? That is indeed a challenge. Faith is put to the test in all sorts of new ways.

Nearer to many is the experience of change within the culture that is known and familiar. We live in a world of change, and on the whole we are not very good at coping with change. For comfort, change needs to come slowly. It is helpful to have good warning. Good management will introduce change slowly and with much consultation. Keep every one in the picture.

Think about the institution of the Church of England. For those who worship in their parish church, there is often resistance to change. For those of you who may watch *Miss Marple, Heartbeat*, or *The Royal*, what is it that you like about them? Is it the stability of the known? In *Miss Marple*, the idyllic English country village provides a backdrop that is known and comfortable to many. The bells are rung in the village church; the vicar provides the people with his weekly sermon and comforts the elderly and ill. There is time for the niceties of life. Time for that cup of tea and meals are, of course, taken at the table. Members of the Parochial Church Council (PCC) are not fed with papers that talk of change and warnings about fewer vicars being available. That would be unthinkable. The church and the vicar are part of the routine of the English village way of life, part of the culture.

Add the individual's spiritual needs to the changing face of the Church of England, and you have quite a high level of discomfort. This is not, therefore, entirely about God – it is about the comfort zones in which we worship and share that side of ourselves with others.

In the sixties, a number of Asian people had to leave a certain country in Africa. The circumstances in which they left were difficult. Some settled within the United Kingdom. Hard working and diligent, they made a new life for themselves, but how much they had to leave behind. When I was talking to a man who is now in his fifties about that time, he remarked upon the feeling of being uprooted in a violent way. There had been no time to say goodbye. His feelings at the time as a teenager were intense and hitherto unknown to him. He had never experienced the intensity of emotions before that time.

Anyone who has been sent away to school and has experienced the feeling of being homesick will begin to touch on and understand the feelings experienced by that man. It hurt. A deep pit of feeling sick stayed with him for months. He felt disorientated and ill at ease. He felt vulnerable, frightened, and was always looking over his shoulder for danger. As the grown-ups in his life struggled to make a new home, he stayed close to them and was afraid of all the new sights and smells and colours. England was grey. The food was tasteless. He seldom remembered feeling warm and began to wonder if there was sunshine. Slowly and painfully, he began to find his feet. As he mixed with other boys, he knew he was different. On one hand, he was proud of his difference, yet that difference made life so painful for him. He missed the warmth, the sound of the different languages, the smiling faces, the familiar food, and the smell of home. Bit by bit his family found their feet, and so did he. They created a new safe home for themselves. They began to lay the foundations for what made them, with their culture, feel at home.

Years later he returned for a visit to the country of his birth. He made the journey back by plane. The plane flew by night. Throughout the night, he was unable to sleep. The sense of anticipation gripped him. He felt close to tears much of the time. As the plane came to land, he experienced a great sweep of emotion. Tears fell down his face. His hands were clenched. He felt himself holding his breath. This was not because he was afraid of landing; it was because of where he was landing. The wait in the plane after landing and before he was able to step onto land took an eternity. Then down the steps he went. The sun beat down upon him, the warm air encompassed him, and he felt drowned and intoxicated by the smell and feel of it all. It was as if he was wrapped in a blanket of welcome. The tears poured down his cheeks, and unashamedly he fell to his knees and kissed the land on which he stood.

It seems that every visit that he has made since then has been packed with the same sort of emotions. One cannot easily explain why. It just is so. There are many others who can relate such stories. Those who travel back to the place of their birth where they had their very identity moulded into their inner being experience the 'sinking into the armchair' feeling in airports all over the world.

Many out there in the world will know of such an experience, and for some it is still to come. Be gentle with yourself. If you have been uprooted, it really helps to be with others who have had the same experience. That is how many have coped over the years. If you are not actually living with others in this situation, then getting together from time to time is so valuable.

One woman I know, a mother of three children all born in England, shut herself off from the intense feelings that she had for Africa when she left there as a child. For all that she did return from time to time, it always hurt so much. She did not feel that she fitted into either place, the country of her birth or the country where she now lived. When she was in Africa, she felt different. She felt an outsider looking in, for all that every place that she went to was packed full of memories. When she returned to England, she felt different. She did not have a bank of memories to draw on. She did not fully fit.

She lived like this for years and could not even begin to express the pain that she had locked away deep inside her. That pain was very occasionally expressed when alone, as she looked at pictures of the land and the people that she loved. Tears then came, soon to be wiped away with the emotions. When other people spoke of the land that she loved and knew so well, she simply shut off. They were on forbidden ground for her emotions. They had not lived and cried for that country as she had over the years. They had not seen birth and death of family members in that land. Their understanding was that of someone looking in objectively and taking in the people and the places with the interest of a traveller. Quite permissible, but it did not sit well with her.

Healing only came when she was able to take her children back to that continent and watch them experience the sheer wonder of Africa. Together they felt the heat, watched the sunset, listened to the sounds of the night, ate the food, and drank the beer.

Together they climbed into a single engine plane, the only other person on board being the pilot. The plane shuddered and spluttered and then, with a surge of power took off into the sky. They looked down over the landscape of Africa. As they neared their destination; a small island in the middle of a vast lake; the plane swooped low over the brown, animal-scattered landscape. The tiny plane bumped and landed in a cloud of fine, brown dust. The dust of Africa lay upon them all. They all stood on that wonderful, brown airstrip. They gazed at the trees, the scrub, and the stray animals on the edge of the brown. The smell of wood-smoke greeted them. They breathed in the sun and the dust and the air. Dusty wind blew in her face and ruffled the mother's hair. Something connected. The warmth of Africa enveloped her. Every part of her seemed wrapped in the smell, the sound, the dust, and the joy and pain of Africa. She stood rooted to the spot.

She looked at her children as they gazed in wonderment at Africa. And then she laughed. The mother laughed, and in that laugh she embraced her children into the very essence that is Africa. She laughed and delighted in it all and her body came to life. Her feet tingled as they touched the land. Holding on to the youngest child, she walked forward with the other two children by her side. As they walked, a song of Africa came to mind and she hummed. Some deep sort of connection had occurred within that mother. In some inexplicable way, the years of closed sadness and sorrow she had experienced were blown away, and an understanding as to the essence of Africa had been forged between the mother and her children.

The whirling dust of Africa became a whirling dance in her heart, and the sights and smells of that great continent replaced the mourning in the heart. Her heart felt like it would burst. She could laugh again with the swirling dust, the very stuff that made that land. It was about connection with her offspring as she stood on the earth upon which she had taken her own first steps.

She tells me that it still hurts, but there is now a memory forever etched into her heart. She had shared Africa with her children. She had shared her roots with them.

If you are touched with any of these thoughts, know that you are not alone and know that one's culture is part of one's very being. Do not be ashamed of it.

Times change and we have to move, some in a geographical manner, some in ways and customs. Life moves on, moves forward into new experiences and places and people. Be secure in that 'inner you'. No one can take that from you, and it is yours forever. It is the base from which you grow. It is a good base because it belongs to you.

If you experience great pain as you think about such matters, do talk about it. For elderly people, the world can seem so full of change and discomfort. Yes, the old days for many were the best. That is why it is so good to look back and hold onto what has made up your life. What has shaped and moulded you?

For most, the moulding of the past is what gets them through the present. But for some, they are stuck in the memories and the people of the past. It is understandable, especially if the past has been so rich and so full of life and love. Your every fibre longs for the people who made those memories with you.

When you are hurting, do talk to someone. Tell them your story. Tell them what is hurting. Let the emotions come and express your feelings. Talking can help to build that transition bridge. At least, it will feel more comfortable, at best, you will be all the stronger as you take in the past and encounter the new, strong in your culture. If you are strong, you will not want to diminish the richness of the culture in which you live. Breathe it in, and it will continue to form you.

There is richness in diversity, and you can own that richness as you mix the traditional with new ways. As you journey, hold onto the inner you. You will then be secure and able to embrace new ways of doing things, if that is what is asked of you.

Chapter Seven

The Hurting Inner Child

Finding the Void and Starting the Process of

Healing

I mentioned having a box of tools early on in this book. As I work, I am armed with this tool kit. I need to consider the right way to help each individual. That will depend upon their situation and their view of life. I try to respond to the whole of them. To offer healing that involves and engages with body, mind, and spirit. I find that the process not only changes the mind and body, but also touches the spirit in some mysterious way.

There are a range of counselling models; counsellors will be trained in, and will work with, their preferred model. To follow the process of counselling will lead the counsellor and your client forward. The quest is to find the void. Once found, it will be an unravelling of thoughts, actions, feelings and emotions. Past behaviour will begin to make sense as will the present feelings. Pieces of the jigsaw puzzle will be found.

Because of my background, I am familiar with the Christian approach regarding prayer for healing not only in the form of prayers offered within a church setting, but also through prayer ministry, which is more structured, as well as 'The Healing of the Family Tree'. The latter is valuable in the right setting but may cause harm if used in isolation without regard to what makes up the whole. Too often I listen to people who have received 'counselling' from well-meaning people and who received prayer from the same people. This is not counselling as those of us who are professional with many years of training in our field see it.

When listening to people who have received such 'counselling', I hear about words that have been 'put on them' during prayer times. They have been left feeling distressed and far from whole. Especially damaging are words indicating that the person has some sort of evil spirit within. A prayer for deliverance then follows this suggestion. Much damage can be, and indeed, has been done by well meaning people.

To clarify my position, it may be helpful to offer that I have been involved in the ministry of healing for some thirty years. I have been a part of excellent practice in our churches and cathedrals in different parts of the country, and have received training and insight from well-respected people such as Bishop Morris Maddocks, Francis MacNutt, Kenneth MacAll, Russ Parker, and John Woolmer. I have also been to large Christian conferences where prayer for healing was offered and have been an observer, a receiver, and a member of the ministry team.

Visiting other parts of the world, I have seen startling things occur. I acknowledge the power and negative impact upon an individual when things of a dark and evil nature occur. This being said, we do have to be very sure as to the root of the problem. What may be seen as something not of God may in fact be an expression of fear, or indeed is part of the presenting imbalance of a mental health issue.

I have been privileged to have been witness to times of great movements of the Holy Spirit and have seen healing take place in an awe-inspiring way in three different countries: Malawi, Canada and England. This is the sort of power that can lead onto revival, but that is for another book. I cannot explain why the power of God through his Holy Spirit breaks forth in such a way from time to time, but I know it to be true. For the most part, we don't experience such visible acts. We move forward with expectation and good practice. We are indeed most wonderfully made – body, mind, and spirit. All parts need to find the right balance. My desire is to understand the potential dangers if we do not respect the complexities of each individual and simply plough into well-meaning prayer and 'counselling'. This can cause much damage.

That being said, how do we heal that empty, hurting space? Here we have a variety of options. This will vary for both the individual and the therapist, depending upon the background. I can offer how it has worked for me in my practice as a therapist, and also as one who has seen and experienced the power and effectiveness of other tools such as prayer ministry and 'The Healing of the Family Tree'.

Firstly, I listen. Really listen. We all have our story. That story is unique to each one of us. It is essential to hear the story as presented by the individual. This is what takes place in the room as the individual shares his or her story with me. I listen to the words, hear how they are spoken and with what emotion and feeling they are conveyed. I watch and wait and allow the silences and the body language to speak to me. I encourage and convey my respect for the person who trusts me to enter into their journey of discovery. The story will unfold over the weeks. It may change, and that is all part of the unfolding of the story. The sum total of the individual consists of body, mind, and spirit. Feelings and emotions straddle the mind and body, and each person brings with them their spiritual being.

As the therapist, I work with the hurting individual to help them to reach a point of understanding, which will then lead on. That point of understanding will then require different actions from me, and from the one who seeks help. We dig deeply into the toolbox. Reaching a state of acknowledgement and acceptance for what has taken place in the individual's life is a major step. Facing the void and the hurt and 'owning' what has been discovered is a revelation for the individual. I tread with care. These are delicate times for the individual. They will be vulnerable and will be experiencing a range of emotions. It is one thing to say yes this happened. How might their lives have changed as a result of this happening or happenings? It could well be a series of events from the past and then one event that triggers the need to seek help. One may be looking at a lifetime of defence walls that have been built in order to survive.

The individual will not see it as survival, since it has become the normal mode of operation for that individual. Once they have begun to accept past issues, they may well swing into different forms of denial. The acceptance may be too much, and there may be a backing off to then be able to 'own' a little more. This is about helping them to find a way forward. It is a process of letting go in order to seek a new way to journey, freed up from things of the past.

So, having reached the point of acceptance, we start to look at how it feels and how it has impacted on their behaviour and relationships. This is delicate work to say the least. To have a knowledge and understanding of how the mind works is crucial. Starting to help another to look back and face past issues is not to be done in anything but a very structured and safe, professional manner. For some, changing how they view life is, in their eyes, just not possible. They are fixed in their 'safe' way of living, even if that way is limiting their actions and relationships. Respect must be observed at all times for the individual, along with support and unconditional positive regard. The therapist offers a safe setting for the individual. Confidentiality is crucial. The individual is then in a safe setting to work with the therapist.

As we move forward, we work with the pain, the fear, the anger, the guilt, the distress, the disbelief, perhaps the shock, and the denial. We discover that hurting void full of emotional loss. You may note that the emotions that I have mentioned are often cited following the death of a loved one. This is when I know that we have reached the void that started the person on their voyage of discovery.

What tools will be used to find release? Please keep in mind the holistic approach. As I work with each person, once we have grasped and 'owned' what is in the void, I consider the most appropriate 'tools' that will enable that person to reach the point of release. What is perfect for one is certainly not for another. People usually understand that pain from the past may well touch the body as well as the mind. Then, as we considered earlier in this book, most people seem to accept that there is a force higher than them. This being the case, consideration of how they may be helped in this area, how their spirit may be hurting, is also talked about, and a package of care leading to healing and release is formulated within the sessions.

To Clarify

All that we have looked at so far has now brought us to the point of thinking and looking at inner hurts that may be found deep inside us. This area is about the damage that has happened to us, either intentionally or through circumstances of life, that has 'wounded' us in some way during the course of our life.

What points us to the need for help in this area? Depression, anxiety, some sort of eating disorder, difficulty in sleep, grief and loneliness, and so on are all factors that lead people to a point of seeking help. Some say they feel held down in life. They may be unable to reach out for life as they would like to do. Something is preventing them from living life in all abundance. Upon further enquiries, the story begins to unfold.

They are held back from the fullness of life by a range of feelings that are unwanted and, in many cases, are most uncomfortable. At worst, these are having a considerable impact upon the individual such that their lifestyle is ruled by the strength of the feelings and emotions.

They may start to describe fears, anxieties, and compulsive behaviour, or talk of feeling depressed, or describe how they have erratic fits of anger. They may have to live their lives to a specific pattern because that is the only safe way.

What they are talking about is the damaged inner self. We are now looking at the need for inner healing. As we do so, the individual is encouraged to recall and then to work through painful times in their lives that have left a scar, an inner hurt that will not go away and that many years on, still stays with them. The inner hurt may have caused the symptoms that the person describes. Inner healing is thus about ministering to damaged emotions and unhealed memories.

It is accepted that we all have knocks in life.

Those knocks start when we are very vulnerable and continue until old age and on to death. Life is a journey from the point of conception, and the moment a baby is born he or she must begin to struggle to survive. They draw their first breath and yell, and their basic instinct to suck swings into place. That is the start of the life journey. We learn how to cope with the good and the not-so-good parts of life. Depending upon the circumstances, for some people the not-so-good bits of life become a weight in some way. For whatever reason, the individual is unable to deal with the hurt, to learn and grow from it and then let it go. They are not able to process that pain, be it of body, mind, or spirit. It is when the recovery part within each one of us is unable to swing into action that we have the problems. This is how we come to the point of needing inner healing.

So How Has It Been for You? Let Us Journey through Your Childhood

How did you start life? Life, of course, does not start at birth. It begins at conception. You then have your journey within the womb. Both conception and birth are very important in the formation of the inner you. Was the time of conception full of love and joy and anticipation? Or was it amid a haze of alcohol and noise and even violence? Was the news of your mother's pregnancy greeted with excitement and great anticipation or was it dreaded news that had to be faced?

The same goes for your birth. How was it for you?

Were you a twin or one of even more? Did you have an easy birth or was it traumatic, full of tension? Were you born in hospital or at home or even somewhere else? Who was with you at the point of birth? Who were the people in your life in your early years? Clearly the answers to these and other similar questions will be different for us all. A child who has been adopted will have a very different story to tell from the child born at home surrounded by father, granny, and older siblings. Do you have any pictures of yourself as an infant? Such photographs can be quite revealing.

At this stage in life, it may not be any specific actions taken against us that cause damage. It is more a case of simply being caught up and involved in a set of circumstances; circumstances that may have caused hurt within.

Experiences that are out of our control – indeed conception and birth fall into this category – may lead to an anxious feeling, a feeling of being isolated and helpless in a hostile world.

CASE STUDY: Edith

Edith is a woman in her mid-eighties. She came for help because she was anxious about going into hospital for an operation. It seemed that her fear was not about the operation but about being 'shut away' in hospital. As we talked, it transpired that she also suffers from migraines and is unable to cope with enclosed spaces. To counter this fear of being shut away, enjoying very good health until this point, she had ensured that she was able to get out into the country for long walks on a regular basis. "To fill my lungs with air," she told me. I asked her how she felt if she did not go for these walks, and she described feeling trapped and said that the fear of being trapped triggered a migraine.

I began to ask her about her start in life. She thought it very strange to look back over so many years. It turned out that she was born in Singapore just before the Second World War. As a small infant she, along with her mother and brother, had been rounded up and put into a camp for the duration of the war. She made light of it saying that she was so young that she took it all as quite normal. That was until she told me of things that her mother had related about the cramped living conditions and a long train and truck journey during that period. As she talked, she began to wipe her brow. "It was the heat," she told me. "You felt like you were a sardine in a tin," she went on to say. As she talked more, she realised that she was starting to re-live a journey that she had made in the company of many woman and children through a steamy jungle in a series of modes of transport. She even began to sense the smell of that journey.

Edith believed in God and we discussed at length the place of suffering in the world. She needed to find answers. She had carried the burden of the experiences of her early life with her and she now dared to ask questions. Anger rose within her, it welled up into fury. She had a lifetime of feelings and emotions pushed deep down within her. As she discovered the strength of the emotions, she was at times alarmed, but I was able to reassure her and encourage her to continue and go with the flow. The whole process was a revelation to her. The depth of what she was experiencing amazed her.

Over the following weeks we met and bit by bit she began to own her feelings and emotions. Her past experience as well as her present actions began to come together in some sort of picture. It was like finding pieces of a jigsaw puzzle. God most certainly came into this exploration for her. Without him she could not have made sense of it at all.

It is most important in this work to consider the individual in a holistic way. How each person describes the spiritual side of their lives will vary. I have worked with people of great, little, or no apparent faith (their description of that side of their lives). As we worked in this holistic way, Edith began to be able to see God in her pain. She started to experience release. The need to walk became less, and she was able to get through her hospital stay with relative ease. The process of healing was well on the way.

That is an example of how we may be wounded from early experiences. We may have wounds inflicted upon us inadvertently or quite deliberately. One thinks automatically of physical wounds, but we now understand that we may be wounded in other ways as well. We need to be alert to the fact that wounds may be physical, mental, sexual, emotional or spiritual, or in any combination.

Harm can be done to us but so too may we cause ourselves damage. We make incorrect decisions and damage ourselves through our actions. Life can become complicated through relationships, finance, work, and so on. There is no condemnation when we put our shortfalls on the table. This is the bit about personal responsibility. We have to be willing to take responsibility for our own actions.

To continue this thinking, are you comfortable with your life-style or is it hurting you? You may decide that you do want to make changes. If you have harmed yourself in your way of life, this decision is the point of change. This could be a good point to start talking.

How you move forward at this stage will vary upon your circumstances. For some, they will look for some sort of forgiveness. In this instance it may be that they need to forgive themselves. Some people find this very difficult. When they are able to do so – it may often be a process over a long period of time – they are then able to start on a new pathway.

CASE STUDY: Angela

Angela came to see me in a state of great distress and also shame. She took weeks and weeks to tell me that she had had sex with a man some twenty years previously. This had resulted in her being pregnant. So ashamed was Angela of the next action that was to come, that she spent several more weeks before she told me that she had had an abortion. Angela had held onto these facts for twenty years, and they had become deeply rooted in her body, mind, and spirit. She 'punished' herself in her body by believing her body to be 'unclean' and had cut herself off from any other relationships with men. She lived a rather sad, lonely life on her own as a single woman. Her mind was in turmoil. She really showed much anguish and expressed the guilt that she carried all these years on. Her spirit, too, had suffered. She worked so hard at being a good person to make up for the bad person she felt she'd been. A life of banishment from the world was effectively what had happened to Angela.

Eventually we moved forward together and more and more evolved as we talked. Both her father and her brother had abused Angela as a child. Her mother had expressed shock and anger when she had discovered that Angela was pregnant all those years ago, and the words that she spoke to Angela at that time had never left her. Angela had never 'matched up' to her parent's expectations and lived a very sad life overshadowed by guilt and great loneliness.

She believed that she deserved all that life threw at her from the point when she had sex with the young man. The possibility that there were mitigating circumstances – and indeed what took place would, in my view, be seen as rape – had escaped her thinking. She had lived with her actions of some twenty years ago at such a cost to her life. She read about sexual immorality in the Bible and 'owned' and thus condemned herself. If only she had talked to a professional sooner, she would have been able to see the bigger picture, and life would have been so different. In her case, she was never really able to find full freedom, but she did find a measure of release. It was just too difficult for her to shake away the restricted living that was her life. She had too many walls of solid defence and had crafted her life firmly into the walls. Taking away too many bricks in her wall would have been too frightening. Life is seldom clear cut.

Common Reasons That People Have for Coming for Help

1. Overwhelming feelings

Anxiety, depression, fear, anger, or confusion. Check out with your doctor to ensure that there is not a chemical or hormonal imbalance. But, such feelings may result from hurts received.

2. Guilt

False or real. Real guilt needs to be faced and dealt with in order to find release. False guilt, which is far more common, needs to be explored, and the truth found. It may then be cast into the deep ocean with a 'No fishing' sign put over it.

3. Words and sayings

Some words that may have stayed with you. It is so very damaging to have judgements made on you as a child. They can keep you in a tight trap. They bind you and you believe in them. Your life reflects them. Consider a child who is told such things as: "You are not clever." "You are no good at maths." "You get everything wrong." "If only you were a girl." "You always get it wrong." "You are fat."

If you do have words that have stayed with you, what impact have they had upon you? The possibility is that you will have developed inner vows, sayings that reflect the initial words. "I am useless." "I am just rubbish." "I am so fat." "I don't trust anyone." "I will never cry." "I can do it all on my own." People who remember saying such things to themselves as children very often continue to act out these words in adult life.

4. Physical symptoms

It is acknowledged that some physical problems such as Irritable Bowel Syndrome (IBS), stomach ulcers and migraines may be linked in with our emotional 'baggage'. By 'baggage' I mean past hurtful memories, hurts that have come our way as we have journeyed through life.

Such baggage includes past trauma and past loss in our life. We all carry baggage with us. When we are confronted with hurts and pains, all too often we do not give ourselves time to process the happening that has caused these. That is not to say that every detail of our lives needs to be processed. However, the big events in our lives, which of course include the death of anyone close to us, do need time and consideration and reflection. This is what we know as grief. Other loss situations in our lives also require a period of grief. It gives the body, mind, and spirit time to catch up. The pace of life may be fast but we cannot ignore the need to grieve.

Combined Therapy

If one goes into hospital to have a knee replacement, for instance, the individual will see a number of medical practitioners, all specialists, in their own fields. Initially this will probably be the general practitioner, followed by a visit to the hospital to see the surgeon or one of the team, the pre-admission nurse, and the phlebotomist who takes blood to check that all is well for surgery. Once in hospital, the anaesthetist and nurses, as well as a member of the surgical team, will see the patient before surgery. The surgery completed, there will be still more people offering their services to help the patient along, including the physiotherapist. The physiotherapist will continue to feature in the patient's life as they start to move and exercise the new joint. The physical wellbeing of the patient is met in careful nursing and hopefully good nutrition. All this helps the healing process. All in all, a great team effort, which will ensure the recovery of the patient.

In the same way, a team approach may be most helpful with matters of the mind. The proviso is that those who offer help are trained and professional in what they offer, with the correct checks and balances to ensure good practice. There are so many alternative-type therapies out there in the market place. The church also offers what may be seen as alternative therapy.

The challenge is to help the church to see the need to have good practice in all that they offer. Sadly, this is not always the case. At the very least, one hopes that love and prayer support from a distance can back the work of any individual who is receiving therapeutic help, just as prayer is offered for anyone undergoing surgery.

Three Areas of Ministry That the Church Can Offer

1. Listening

For many years I have offered a self-awareness and listening course to those who have a desire to help people who are hurting, and who recognise the need to get it right for them. I see the training a little like learning to be a St. John's Ambulance first aider. A first aider can take the initial action, which may be all that is needed. It may be that more help is needed, so they can then 'hold' the individual in a safe place until the ambulance crew arrives.

Listening is an art, and something that is much needed in our fast-moving world. To be really listened to is a healing experience. It does much for the self-worth of the individual. To be a listener is a challenge. We may think that we are listening, but are we? How often do thoughts of our own intrude and mingle with the words of the speaker?

Try sitting with a friend and give each other four minutes to talk about an event that has stayed in your memory. As you listen, note what intrudes into the listening. Do you hear any noises from outside? Does something in the other person's story jog a memory for you? Do you find yourself thinking of that rather than listening?

Each try this exercise and see how it leaves you feeling. Be honest with one another. Think about how you were sitting; did you have eye contact? How did the speaker's voice sound; did it change pitch at any point?

Try this again, but this time, give each other some feedback. What do you think were the key points that were given to you as you listened? Share them with each other and see if you are hearing what the speaker is trying to convey.

As we listen, we do need to be self-aware. Why is this? Things from our past may well hinder us in the process of listening if we have not acknowledged and dealt with them. If we have not worked on our own issues, we may well be tempted to bring in our own story. Listening requires energy. If we need to push down our own story and thus our own emotions all the time, we shall become very exhausted.

Simply wanting to be able to help someone does not mean that you are able to do so without first doing some work upon yourself. Let me explain further. You may have a desire to make a table. However, unless you know about the correct wood, the correct tools and the correct way to set about making the table, you will not make a very good table! You need the knowledge to set out upon such a venture. It is no different with listening in this deep way. So, what tools do we have within us to listen? We simply bring ourselves. We thus need to know ourselves in order to use our inner resources in a constructive way.

However, we must not use our experience of life in such a way that we 'put on others' how we think they may feel because that is how we feel. To be self-aware is crucial in the art of listening. As we become more self-aware, we gain distance from ourselves and so may become more objective as we listen.

Self-Awareness

Here are some questions for you.

- What do you like about yourself?
- How do you feel about yourself in the family role?
- What are your creative accomplishments? Here we are thinking about music, art, writing, and so on.
- What are your good physical features? Your smile, your eyes, your hands.
- Have you changed over the past five years?
- Have you overcome any fears in the past five years?
- What were the bad patches in your life (e.g., school, college, marriage, a certain job, etc)?
- How are you with regard to feelings and emotions? Do you express them, push them down, or are you frightened of them?

You may discover that some of these questions are difficult to answer and, indeed, some of them may raise issues for you. If this is so, do consider taking it further. If you want to be a listener, you will certainly need to work on your self-awareness.

A listening course may offer a firm foundation upon which to build a pastoral care team within a church. Many a team has been built as a result of such a course. But that is not the end. Just as professionals have to give evidence of continued training, so too should individuals who are part of a pastoral team. The initial course will be the step-off point. Once the work of listening starts, there must be provision made for feedback and discussion. Of course, confidentiality is a factor to be considered. It is possible to maintain confidentiality and still be able to discuss issues. Such a group will need a facilitator. This person will need to have received more than the basic listening course. It is important also to check on how the listeners are feeling themselves. The most usual problem is when a listener takes on the feelings and emotions of the speaker and becomes pulled down by the burden.

2. Prayer

People have looked to prayer for many generations. Prayer for healing has been a recognised ministry in the church and, indeed, some churches have specific healing services whereby identified people pray with individuals as needed. Many find great comfort and help in the act of asking for, and receiving, prayer.

Prayer ministry is different from offering prayer

within the context of a church service. The thinking behind prayer ministry is that God knows our deepest needs and if we wait on him in prayer, we shall be prompted to find our way forward.

Such a ministry is structured in that a church will have formed a prayer ministry team. Working in pairs, they should have received good training, which would most certainly include a course on self-awareness and listening skills. I emphasise the need to train those who offer this ministry. Just as with a listening pastoral team, the team who offer prayer ministry will need careful supervision and on-going training. I have seen prayer ministry happen in several churches. Where there was safe practice, it was most helpful. Where there was not the training, and thus the supervision, it came to a grinding halt after some time and left hurt people in its wake.

Prayer ministry courses are available. The best practice is that such a course will be offered at the request of the church leader and so have the full backing of the leadership.

3. Healing of the Family Tree

This is another tool in the toolbox that may be used. The thinking behind this can be found in a book, 'Healing the Family Tree' by Kenneth McAll, M.D. (McAll *A Guide to Healing the Family Tree* 1994 The Handsel Press Ltd). This book is for any who are interested in learning about ancestral healing. Kenneth McAll is the foremost authority in this area. A psychiatrist, he addresses the area of what might have been passed on from one generation to another and how things from the past may affect the present. In our family history, we may discover that there have been traumas such as suicide or murder, abortion, miscarriage, family feuds, and so on.

This is not about blame. It is about understanding difficulties that may have been passed on through the generations. McAll looks at how events and situations that have happened in the past can impact our lives and the places where we live in the present. Put into the context of family tree ministry, this may be most effective.

I listened to Kenneth McAll for a week when he spoke at Lee Abbey in Devon. I have also been able to work alongside clergy who have taken onboard the thinking behind this area, and have seen how individuals and families may find release following such help. Dr. David Wells and Stephen Baker have written other helpful books on this subject. Both of these books are available via the author of this book.

This ministry (or one could substitute 'therapy' for ministry) needs careful preparation. As a therapist, from time to time but not often, it seems that such a ministry would be helpful to an individual, and if appropriate I use this. In this setting, and of course with their consent, we work through a series of questions that look at their family history. People often say they do not know much of their past, but as they warm to it they realise that they do indeed know more than they thought. Some produce a family tree. What we are looking for will be events, situations, actions, and emotional impacts that have taken place within a family. So, for instance, a drowning at sea, a murder, drug abuse, and so on all add to the list of things that have come through the generations. They would all come under the list of losses that I have talked about in earlier chapters. It is important to take one's time as one works on the family tree. Old family photos can be helpful. The check sheet is vital as it prompts the individual to think about areas not ever considered before.

One then moves forward one stage; as the therapist, one helps the individual to see that all that has gone before is part of their story. They are not responsible for the things – good or bad – that have taken place, but they are part of what has come before them. Having embraced this thinking, we move to the next stage.

We know the saying: "The sins of the fathers are visited on the children." This means just what I have already suggested. Past events all too easily impact on the present. This next stage is about embracing all that is part of the person's 'story' and in effect saying 'sorry' to God for it. I hasten to add that this is not about blame. It is very matter-of-fact. 'This happened in my family and it has left a legacy. I am sorry and would like this legacy to stop now, so that as a family we are no longer affected by it' is the sort of thinking. Put another way, one is asking for forgiveness and release for things of the past.

The last stage is to arrange a service where bread and wine may be shared (in other words, a service of communion). The Church of England has a very good service that can be used. One needs to find a parish priest who is comfortable and knowledgeable in this area, and then the individual and the counsellor and any other family member of the person's choice meet, often in a church. Having attended several such events, I can say how moving and astonishingly effective they can be. The words speak of sorrow for things past, a desire for the past to be forgiven, a prayer for any who have died in tragic or violent actions, and so on. It is like wiping the slate clean in order for the family to move on unencumbered by past issues.

CASE STUDY: Susan

Susan came to me with a range of problems including a very strong fear of death. We then became more specific and it seemed that each generation in the female line had a fear of the death of their mother. The fear was really very strong and made moving on into adulthood difficult for the girls, generation after generation. Eventually I saw three generations of the females in the family, and they all spoke of the same fears and nightmares.

The time came when I suggested family tree ministry. After a good deal of preparation we all met and went through the service with the parish priest. It was very quiet, and I really wondered if anything had happened at all. How wrong I was, for over the next few months all of the female family members told me of the sense of release that they had experienced during and after the service. Their attitudes were also starting to change, and the sense of clinging on to one another faded to be replaced by healthy bonds of releasing love.

Chapter Eight

Final Case Study

Abuse is a much wider topic than we think; hence, I have taken this as my major example of a case study to show how the thinking regarding inner healing may be applied. These are all transferable to the other aspects of loss described in this book.

CASE STUDY: Ruth

Ruth came to seek help. She presented as cheerful but there was nervousness just below the surface. There was urgency in telling her story. She was an incest survivor. As a child, an older brother looked after her.

Her mother was unable to cope. She was on tranquillisers. Her father was an alcoholic.

When Ruth was aged six, her father introduced her to a 'new game'. This game started with touch. He touched her arm, her leg, and her knee. The next time this game was played, his hands went to the intimate parts of her body, and he touched her genitals. When Ruth was aged eight, he had full sex with her.

Throughout this time, he warned Ruth against telling her mother. The fear of her mother knowing was equal to the fear of what her father was doing to her. Ruth froze inside and became numb. She spoke very little and viewed the world through fearful eyes. The abuse continued until Ruth was eleven.

Ruth remembered very little between the ages of eleven and eighteen. Indeed, she had blanked out the events of her childhood to a large degree. This is not uncommon in such situations.

At the age of eighteen, Ruth had a bad accident. She was in hospital for several weeks and during that time she was overwhelmed by the care and kindness that the staff showed to her.

As she lay in hospital, past memories came flooding back to her. As she recovered from her injuries, she found it more and more difficult to live with the flood of memories. She decided that she needed to seek help. Through her GP she saw a counsellor, but the six sessions that were offered to her were not helpful. Ruth then came to see me.

Ruth stated that the past counsellor had only been interested in the 'juicy bits'. She had felt rushed and pressured into talking about the abuse long before it felt safe to do so.

Building up a relationship of trust is all-important. One also needs to acknowledge that it takes determination and courage to face such enormous hurt and pain that comes from such an abusive past.

Thus one starts to build up a relationship of trust. Being there for the person and respecting them by giving time, unconditional positive regard, and acceptance are all crucial.

Points to remember when helping someone like Ruth.

- The giving of time: listen with intent
- Unconditional positive regard: we mean that, by your attitude of listening and response, you convey to her that her story is worth listening to
- Acceptance: accept Ruth for who she is – not how you might like her to be

Insights to help you in the process of listening.

- This is not her fault. The child is always the innocent one. She is not to blame in any way at all.
- Be mindful of her feelings of self-respect and self worth
- Issues of trust. Be aware of the difficulty of trust in such situations. The area of trust will need to be well explored.
- Her feelings of low self-worth may well feed a belief in her that she is not due, or is not worthy of, respect.
- Love – explore what it means to Ruth.
- Look at relationship issues. How has the abuse left Ruth feeling in this area?

Care to be taken in the following areas:

- From the start ensure that you feel able to work with the person who comes for help.
- Be honest, and refer the person if you feel you are not the right therapist for the work.
- Should you refer the person, do so with great care. There is a danger that they may feel rejected and pushed away. Explain that you will find the best possible help.
- Do not break appointments. Work at the individual's pace. Do not promise what is unrealistic.
- Take care with over identification. Do not become overwhelmed emotionally.
- Remember empathic understanding and positive regard at all times.

Checklist within the work

- Believe what the person states – do not try to 'pretty it up'.
- Be firm and strong towards the one who seeks help (client).
- Make a clear contract with client: map out the way you will work.
- Within that suggested way, keep flexible. Listen to God's leading.
- Be sensitive – never cut the person off in mid-speech.
- Encourage the person to write down feelings and experiences. Talk these through in future sessions.

- Community support: find out what support is available to the person (e.g. friends, relatives, church, and other agencies).
- Acceptance – an essential part of the emotional healing process.

Background Knowledge of This Area

An understanding of the realities of sexual abuse is crucial for anyone working with children and young people. As the listener, you need to be totally open to the fact that children are sexually abused. There needs to be knowledge of the complexities of incest (e.g. many children are abused by trusted adults who are not relatives).

There is common consensus that abuse is any exploitation of a child under the age of 16 for the sexual pleasure and gratification of the adult. This ranges from obscene telephone calls, indecent exposure and voyeurism such as watching a child undress, to fondling, taking pornographic pictures, attempted intercourse, rape, incest, or child prostitution. The definition then broadens out into situations when a trusted adult in a position of power and authority takes advantage over a child or young person.

Why Does Incest Happen? Some Facts

Many offenders come from 'normal' family homes, and they tend to be hard-working, devoted family men. The mother may well be unaware of ongoing sexual abuse towards her child. The tell tale signs of abuse are quite often only obvious in retrospect.

Be Aware of the Four Stages in Incestuous Abuse

1. Secrecy

"Everything will be all right if you don't tell." "This is our little game." "It will make everything better." "I feel better for this little chat with you. You help me."

Should the young person want to reveal what is happening, there is a fear of being blamed or not being believed. This happens all too often, especially if the abuse is not hands-on physical sex. This is where the range of abuse needs to be understood.

We need to understand that a certain look, the smile, the body smell, the tone of the voice, the twitching of the lips, the flicking of the hair, the flicking of the ballpoint pen, the pat on the hand and the word of thanks, all done in the same routine at a specific time and place, may well indicate a situation of abuse. Why? Because the young person is left uncomfortable as the weeks turn into months. They feel abused for all that they could not name it at the time.

I have listened to both men and women who recalled car journeys week after week and the little chats that took place within the car. To start with, the times spent with the adult (the mother or father or some other adult) were quite acceptable but, as the weeks wore on, that changed. They felt 'used'. They were being drawn into inappropriate conversations. They were left feeling uneasy, fearful and unsafe.

Young girls are quick to pick up sexual signs. An

unaware man can pass on such signals as he talks. Sadly, such situations may cause problems of trust in the future. The once-trusted male figure, be it the father, uncle, brother, cousin or some other male figure in their life has become unsafe. The girl transfers that level of distrust onto all men in her life and much work will need to be done to change that thinking.

Sexual signals are made in everyday life, but it is how they are made and to whom and in what setting that makes them acceptable or not. During an interview with a convicted abuser the police officer in the room was quick to remove a ballpoint pen that the man was continuously clicking in and out, in and out with a sly smile upon his face. He was making this action as he looked at a young female social worker in the room. His was a game of power, clear for all to see. The power is not always so clear. It is often secret and hidden.

Not being believed is all too common. The mother really cannot believe that her partner or her son would ever abuse her daughter. Should the child begin to indicate that all is not well, there is talk of a child having a 'vivid imagination'.

If there are several girls in the family, the older girl, if she has been abused in the past, will fear for her younger siblings, but she probably will not be able to do anything about it. Who would believe her, and what would happen if she were believed? Would the little sister be taken away? The guilt and the desperate sense of responsibility build up in her mind in a painful way.

Think of the boy who is abused by a father. That child is thrown into total confusion. His role model is doing something to him that shakes him to the core. I have worked with men who, as young boys, were 'touched' by fathers or teachers or other trusted men. The memory has stayed with them, and it is a burden that they carry until it can be released.

It is a fearsome and confused world that these children live in. They may well come to believe that they are responsible for keeping the family together. It is best to stay quiet on all counts, they think. They carry the damage and fear with them into adulthood.

2. Helplessness

A child who does not complain may, quite wrongly, be seen as in some way consenting to the abuse, or at least not being damaged by it. This is quite incorrect.

The adult bears sole responsibility for any sexual activity with a child in whatever form it takes. Children who are abused tend to feign sleep, to shut off, to cope silently.

Early intervention is unusual because of the secrecy and helplessness issues. Children therefore 'accommodate' to the abuse, believing that they must have provoked it or deserved the assaults.

Learning to live with sexual abuse damages children's ability to trust, love, and develop. When working with someone who has been abused, your relationship with him or her is likely to be tested and provoked to prove that trust is impossible. Hold on; building a relationship of trust with them is vital.

3. Delayed, Conflicting and Unconvincing Disclosure

Most ongoing sexual abuse is never disclosed, at least not outside the immediate family. The great danger is that people will assume that the person who does disclose has invented the story. The average adult, including mothers, often cannot believe that a normal, truthful child would tolerate incest without immediately reporting it. It is important to remember that abuse covers a range of behaviour. Those who abuse will often present as pillars of the community. The evidence of those convicted backs up such a statement.

The abuser may not have a diagnosed illness, but if they are convicted, an illness in the form of some personality or mental disorder may well come to light. Treatment is offered to such people. The problem that is faced in 'therapy' is that the abuser is convinced that they are alright and that they certainly have done no wrong.

An abused child of any age may well face an unbelieving audience when she or he speaks of sexual abuse. This is so very painful for them. This is why again and again one observes backtracking after the initial statement. The child, who is at this stage very often a grown up, just cannot face the disbelief of the family. So even as adults, they remain silent.

I have worked with women who have held the secret of abuse for many years. They look back on their lives and lament the loss of any close physical relationships. They still see the family member who abused them as a child, often a brother or a cousin. Their relationship with them is tense with anger not far below the surface. Such situations have a knock-on-effect throughout the family. No one really knows what the problem is, but it is clear that there is unease, discomfort and anger.

<u>4. Retraction</u>

As just stated, the one who speaks of sexual abuse may well change their story because of the reaction at home. They may retract their story and say that the events did not take place. The abused child will feel their action will either preserve or destroy the family – a heavy burden.

Immediate intervention needs to be put into place once the child has talked. The abuser needs to be removed from the situation. The other parent will also need support and a chance to express shock, grief, and anger. That parent will then be better able to support the child.

In the case of an adult 'survivor' speaking out about childhood abuse, it is so important for other family members to know and believe. They, the abused, may not want to believe. For siblings or for the other parent, it will be a shocking revelation. However, if one has eyes to see, there will be evidence in the behaviour of the person. Perhaps all is not well for them in relationships. They may find that intimate sexual relations are difficult. Certain touches will cause them to freeze and so on. After the birth of a child, the adult who has been abused as a child may well not want the parent who abused her to see her children. There is a fierce protective wall put firmly in place, which is understandable. If it is the father who has abused a daughter or daughters, it will be especially difficult for any male siblings to come to terms with the revelation. Again, this is understandable. It is most painful for a young man to accept that his father has abused his sister.

The Way I Would Envisage Working with Ruth

First of all, listen to the 'story'. It is not expected that the individual will go into abuse detail. This will come later as trust is built into the relationship. Even so, the telling of the story will take time and great effort for the client. Tell them that they may feel very tired after a session. Work out with them how they will travel home. Perhaps suggest that they stop for a cup of tea and thus have space before going fully back to their everyday life.

A theme that will be repeated throughout the therapy is that I shall give a clear message to Ruth that she did nothing to cause the abuse.

The Sort of Response That You Might Convey to Ruth

- Thank you for sharing that with me Ruth. It was brave of you.
- You tell me that you are an incest survivor.
- You say that your brother looked after you because your mother could not cope. That was a difficult situation for a six-year-old.

- You tell me that your father is an alcoholic.
- As a child you were faced with a very difficult set of circumstances.
- I wonder how it felt for you at that age.
- Your father then introduced you to this game.
- You remember being undressed and your father being on top of you.
- As a little girl, you felt very uncomfortable. You describe how messy it all seemed. You remember going to the bathroom to clean up.
- You felt shocked by the experience. Your father had just had full sex with you.
- Your first reaction was to tell your mother. When you were brave enough to say that to your father, he told you not to and said that if you did, your mother would hit you.
- Fear of being hit was too great for you. Your father offered you money.
- You were in a quite impossible situation for any child.
- This was all very stressful for you over the next year. You kept quiet and did as your father asked you, not saying anything to your mother.
- What a lonely place for a little girl.
- You talk about locking your memories away. It was the way you coped with what had happened.
- You had to focus on survival for many years, Ruth.
- Then you had an accident and the memories

all came flooding back. That sounds as if it was very frightening.

- You don't say what the accident was, but clearly it had a trigger effect as far as the memories go. So there you were. You had experienced a bad accident on top of all the held in emotions of your childhood.
- I wonder how that felt for you.
- You realized that you needed help and went to a couple of counsellors for help. I am sorry that they were only interested in the 'juicy bits,' as you put it.
- That is distressing for you, Ruth, and I am very sorry that you have been through those experiences in addition to all the other distress.
- Ruth, you have been through a great deal. I am glad that you felt able to try again to seek help. I work with others who have faced issues like you have described. Of course, everyone's story is unique to that person. I shall take what you tell me as just that.
- It is your story and your journey.
- The way I work is very much at your pace. I shall travel with you and guide you step by step through the pain of the memories.
- Unlike your past counselling experiences, we shall not look in any detail at events for some time. This gives you time to feel comfortable and for you to be able to trust me.
- Our relationship is important to you. Trust is needed.

- I shall respect what you tell me and hold your words in total confidence.
- I suggest that we see each other on a weekly basis.
- We need to find a time that is good for you. Think about the pattern of your week and when it would be best for you. It is important that you have time and a safe place for you to go after each session.
- Within the sessions, you will not have to do anything or say anything that you are not comfortable about. This is important. So if I suggest something that does not feel right for that day, please do tell me.
- It is important to me that you tell me how you feel. So while I can offer you the way forward in your situation, you must feel sure as you respond to my suggestions. Never be afraid to ask questions, challenge me, or tell me that something is not comfortable.
- Some of the work that we shall do will feel uncomfortable as the weeks go by. This is why you need to question me and ask me why at any stage. I am with you on your journey and will help and support you as you travel on the road to recovery.
- How does that all sound to you? Would you like to think about it and then, after we have talked a little more, shall we find the best time and day for you and perhaps book in several sessions, so that you know what is happening

over the next month. How does that sound to you for a start?

The counsellor must settle any known, personal, painful childhood material before embarking upon work with clients in the abuse field. Even if work has been done, should repressed material come to the fore when working with a client, this needs to be taken at once to your supervisor.

One way that I check my emotions out is to listen to certain songs. These are songs that I play to my clients but I also listen to them on my own and let my feelings and any memories come. The CD 'Healing Stream' by Lou Lewis (Lou Lewis, Zimrah Music 1987, re-released 2003) is excellent to use with clients. These songs by Lou Lewis are tried and tested.

Having made it clear that you have heard Ruth's story and having thus started to build up a working relationship with her, this is how I would suggest you move forward in the work.

Moving forward in the work with Ruth

1. Find out the core belief that she has about herself.

"I am…" You will encourage Ruth to change that core belief as the weeks go by.

2. Work with emotions and feelings.

Explain how the two work side by side. Together, look at any negative feelings that Ruth holds. Then start to get in touch with the emotions that come from these feelings.

3. Suggest that Ruth writes thoughts down in between sessions.

This is often very helpful for the individual to do. Within this work we aim to bring the feelings and the emotions into the light. Writing them down makes them real. Talking about them then takes away some of the strength and the hold that they have within the person.

Take all this work at the pace that is good for the individual. You want to avoid Ruth feeling emotionally overwhelmed. She might then feel reluctant to go further. Also keep in mind that Ruth has learned to live within her restrictions. She will have built up strategies and defences. These cannot be taken away from her until the space is filled with positive safe ways.

4. It is good for the individual to either write, or speak out, what they would like to say to the person who

abused them.

This is slow work and is best done in stages. It may be that we think first of the period when the individual was aged between five and seven years. Spend as much time as is needed. Look at any photographs from this time. Remember holidays, birthdays, people who were in that person's life, perhaps family pets. As you do so, help the person to recall the feelings and emotions that were in the life of that small child. People usually find this difficult. Take it slowly and let the person engage and ponder upon the circumstances at that time.

5. When you have worked through these areas, I suggest that they write a letter to themselves at that age. This is a powerful exercise and bears great fruit. Ask them to read out the letter when they next come to you. Hold them in the emotion of the words. Give them time to work through the words that they wrote.

6. At the right time, I move them on to inner child work, which can take a variety of forms. The aim is to help the adult to be in touch with their child. The hurting child needs to be taken into the care of the adult. The adult will then love that little person, and the healing will be like a melting of the two. The hurts of the inner child will melt away.

Working with abuse presents a great challenge regarding boundaries. In such work, keeping the boundaries is vital. Emotions are being discovered and expressed. The counsellor must stay and journey with the client at that point of time. This is where the counsellor needs to be very self-aware so as to hold on with the client without being swamped by the emotions that the client is experiencing. It is a fine but crucial boundary.

Conclusion

As can be seen from the preceding chapters, a void in your life can come in many and varied ways. It may be through ill health, some criminal action, a premature death of some kind, a failed relationship for whatever reason, or your cultural roots being uprooted. Loss is a common denominator.

Reading this book may well spark off a train of thought. You might find a void in your life. It may not be one listed in this book. That is good. The thinking behind this book is precisely to spark off memories and to help you to face the void(s) in your life. Once faced, you may then work with them and come through them with understanding, healing, and peace. This will enable you to live life to the fullest and be at peace with yourself and those around you.

As therapists and carers we are learning all the time. Our objective is to help the hurting by offering safe, therapeutic practice. Nothing short of this is acceptable, for we help the most vulnerable. Belonging to a professional body will provide a code of ethics and ensure accountability and best practice. Part of this best practice will include supervision of our work as well as ongoing training. Listed below are two such professional organisations.

To all who read this book: journey well and be kind to your self.

Association of Christian Counsellors - ACC
29 Momus Boulevard,
Coventry, CV2 5NA,
England
Telephone 0845 124 9569
or 0845 124 9570

British Association for Counselling and
Psychotherapy - BACP
BACP House, 15 St John's Business Park,
Lutterworth,
Leicestershire LE17 4HB,
Telephone - 01455 883300

To obtain copies of 'Healing Stream' by Lou Lewis
contact Lou Lewis, 39 Union Road, Exeter EX4 6HU

For further information, feedback or copies of this
book
Email the author at: info@findacounselloronline.
co.uk
Or via the website http://www.findacounselloronline.
co.uk/

About the Author

Wendy Haslam BA. ED, BA Counselling, Dip CPC

Wendy was born in Africa where she lived as a child in Zimbabwe and Tanzania. She was educated in England and America. She married and lived in Malawi and then the UK with her three children. Wendy came to faith while living in Malawi and also experienced physical healing. This was the start of her understanding as to the breadth of healing which embraces body, mind and spirit.

Building on these experiences she undertook psychological and counselling training and was employed in the NHS (National Health Service) in the UK. Following on from this she has developed her own counselling and therapeutic practice. Currently she is Director of 'Still Waters', an organization offering a breadth of therapeutic practice and training. She is in demand as a conference speaker.

Lightning Source UK Ltd.
Milton Keynes UK
14 October 2010

161264UK00001B/9/P